What was Jesus thinking when he was six years old?

based on a true story

This book is dedicated to my daughters:

Amanda , Wendy , Jill , Tess , and Rita.

I could not be more proud of your accomplishments and the way you have turned out. You know that anything worth anything takes time and hard work. You are my best friends and the lights of my life. Yes, I do have a favorite...and you know who you are.

I especially want to thank my wife, Jennifer, who has encouraged me and supported me through some crazy ideas and experiences. Someday we will get our ticket out of here; I promise you.

I want to thank my mom and dad for raising me to think for myself.

Finally, this book is for Frank and Sam, the greatest grandfathers any kid could ever have...I miss you so much.

Table of Contents

Chapter 1
The Bully

My cousin Simeon pounded his finger hard on the center of my chest. His face was red, and his teeth were clenched. In his anger he managed a muted warning. "Look here Jesus; if you so much as peep when your mom comes in, I'll give you a beating you'll never forget."

My mom did come in. She had to. She heard me pleading for mercy from down the hall and I knew she would wonder what was happening. Looking first at Simeon, she asked, "What's going on, boys? Why all the noise?"

"Aww, nothing, Aunt Mary," Simeon lied. "Jesus and I were just having a little fun. We'll settle down now. Sorry."

My mom looked unconvinced. She glanced from Simeon to me. "You okay, Jesus?" she asked.

"Yeah, I'm fine," I said.

Mom frowned at the two of us. "You boys be careful," she said, leaving the room and returning to her housework.

Simeon looked at me and scowled. "Why, you little pipsqueak. The next time you cry to get your mom's attention, I'll really give you something to cry about."

Simeon was three years older than me, but twice my size. I felt sorry for him. His dad left home when he was just a baby and his mom was rarely around. He survived pretty much on his own and he did this by being tough. He intimidated people into giving him what he wanted and if they hesitated in the least, he usually resorted to violence. Let's face it, he was a bully. But he was my cousin, and I learned to do what he wanted me to. If I didn't, I usually went home with sore ribs and bruises. But something inside me made me pity him. I should have been mad. I should have wanted revenge. But I didn't. At the time, I didn't know why. Now I do.

I was six, almost seven, when Simeon gave me that pounding. It's the first thing in my life I can remember. A lot of people will tell you the first thing they can remember in life is their mom holding their hand on a walk, or their dad giving them a ride on his shoulders, but not me. I remember getting beat up by Simeon. But more than that, I remember how I never hated him for it. In fact, looking back, I remember my reaction to his beatings being more vivid than the blows themselves. I recall that even while getting the stuffing knocked out of me, I felt love for him. I felt sorry for him. I wanted to help him.

One day, several months later, Simeon and I came across an old man, slowly walking down a narrow, secluded path near my home. Simeon's first reaction to seeing this easy prey was to mutter, "Looks like I'm going to get a few shekels today, eh Jesus?" as he moved toward the vulnerable old man.

"Wait, Simeon," I said. "Maybe just once you could help instead of hurt. Please, just this once, can you resist robbing someone and just let me talk to him?"

Simeon looked at me like I was crazy. "What! And pass up an easy heist?"

"Please, just this once?" I begged. "Plus, he's old, and he won't be that fun for you to beat up anyway. Just let me talk to him and see if we can help him out instead."

To this day, I'm still amazed that he agreed. As soon as he uttered, "Okay, do it your way," I raced over to where the old man was walking. "Hi," I said, "my name's Jesus, and my friend here is Simeon. We saw you walking slowly and were wondering if there was anything we could do to help you out?"

The tired old man looked up and started to smile. "Yes there is, boys," his voice low and raspy. "I live down by the river, and I need some help carrying this bag of food. I can't get around very well, and it looks like I bought a bit more at the market than I'm able to carry."

He pulled back his cloak and revealed a large net-like sack filled with melons, onions, potatoes, and some wine. He then looked at Simeon's size and rightly assumed that he would have no problem whatsoever carrying this heavy load. "Here, young man," he said, lifting the bag toward Simeon. "If you can carry this, I'd be very grateful."

I saw Simeon's eyes dart from the bag to me. He was being handed a bundle of goods that was worth at least a week's wages. I knew he wanted to run, take the items with him, and leave the old man with nothing. I clenched my teeth and bore my eyes into his, slowly shaking my head, "No."

For some reason Simeon didn't run. Instead, he turned and walked behind me and the old man all the way to his house. Once there, Simeon placed the food on his table, and the two of us turned to go.

"Wait," the old man said, "this is for you boys."

Reaching into his tunic, he pulled out two shiny gold pieces. Our eyes almost bugged out of our heads. These gold coins were worth at least a hundred shekels each. Handing them over to us, he repeated his thanks.

"I really want to thank you boys for helping me. I was afraid someone might rob me on my way home. I'm so glad I ran into someone I could trust."

On our way home, Simeon was silent. I decided to break the ice. "So, let's see," I said with a bit of a sarcastic grin. "If you would have stolen that old man's bag of food, you would have something worth about ten shekels right now. But instead, you have something worth a hundred. Maybe being nice isn't so bad after all, eh?"

Simeon didn't say a word so I continued. "Plus, stealing the ten shekels worth of food would have also come at a price to your conscience. Now, instead of feeling like dirt for stealing from an old man, you are feeling good about yourself. Simeon, let me ask you a question: when was the last time you felt good about yourself?"

"Shut up, Jesus," he shot back. "If I would have robbed him in the first place, I would have gotten the food, and all of his money. Now I only have one hundred shekels when I could have had two."

I was stunned. This bully was never satisfied. I let him walk a few steps in front of me and I shouted angrily. "I can't speak for the food that you don't have, but if it's the money you want then here." I reached into my pocket and grabbed the gold coin and, threw it at his feet. I shouted, "You're a bully Simeon; a greedy bully. And someday you are going to regret the hurt you have caused me and everyone else."

I turned and left. Walking home alone, I started to cry. I didn't cry because I had just thrown away a hundred shekels. I cried for Simeon. I cried because his greed and envy was killing him from the inside out. I realized then that even though some people looked strong and tough on the outside, if they were filled with hate, they were some of the most miserable people in the world.

When I got home, I told my mom what had happened. She wiped my tears and said that I did the right thing. One hundred shekels would have come in handy at our house for sure, but she assured me that giving the money to Simeon (well, throwing it at him) was probably the right thing to do.

"When Simeon is done spending all that money on himself, he will look back and realize how selfish he was. He will regret this behavior, and say he is sorry. You'll see."

Mom's gentle voice was soothing and reassuring. But deep down, I remembered the evil look in Simeon's eyes, and I knew that this kind of hate was powerful—in fact, maybe the most powerful force on earth.

Chapter 2
The Rabbi

On and on, he droned. It was sweltering hot in our classroom and, quite frankly, my mind was starting to wander. Rabbi Friedman had been lecturing for what seemed like days and all I could think of was taking a cool dip in Decoma Creek as soon as class let out. Then something he said struck a chord. "According to the Prophets, the Messiah is going to come from Nazareth."

For the first time that day, my ears perked up. Perhaps I was just looking for something to find interesting in Rabbi Friedman's lecture until class let out, or maybe I was just curious, but I remember thinking to myself, "Hey, we're all from Nazareth." Raising my hand, I asked the Rabbi a question.

"There are many of us here from Nazareth, good teacher. Do you think one of us might be the Messiah?"

The room erupted in laughter. Some boy shouted, "Hey, maybe it's me!" Others mocked by bowing and pretending to worship him. The Rabbi was furious. He slammed his hand on his desk in an effort to bring an end to this sudden eruption of tom-foolery. Visibly angry with my question, and the other student's response to it, he stared straight at me.

"Do you think you're funny, Jesus?" he asked. "Do you think that being the Messiah is something to joke about?"

"No sir," I responded.

"Well, all right then," he quipped. "I'll have no more of that kind of talk," he said, turning back to his lecture notes.

"But I wasn't joking,"

At this point the classroom went dead quiet and I felt the tension in the room rise rapidly. "What did you say?" the Rabbi said, glaring straight at me and visibly angry at my attempt to challenge him this way.

My heart raced. I felt my throat go tight. My mind filled with fear, but I just had to ask again. "I said, I wasn't joking. Do you think one of us might be the Messiah?"

No one moved, not even the Rabbi Friedman. He just stood there. Our eyes were locked on each other and I could tell he was not sure whether to take me outside and give my backside the switch or answer the question on the table. Thankfully for me it turned out to be the latter. After breathing in deeply, he let out a long sigh.

"Okay, since you seem to have asked a legitimate question, I'll give you a straight answer. Yes, I suppose it is possible that one of you boys could be the Messiah. However, with the way you've all have been behaving, I'd say it's highly doubtful."

He looked at me and could see that I was hurt.

"What's the matter now, Jesus, did you actually think that you might have been the Messiah?" he said in a mocking tone.

"No, not at all sir," I responded. "It's just that you said that the way we have been behaving told you it was highly doubtful, and that really hurt. Can you tell me what I have done, other than perhaps ask you this question today, that would count as bad behavior?"

Rabbi Friedman frowned, and then shook his head. "I'm sorry," he said. "I didn't mean it that way. No, quite frankly Jesus, you have been a model student. All of you boys are good students. I'm sorry, I shouldn't have reacted like that."

He seemed genuinely contrite and I felt sorry for him. It was every Rabbi's dream for the last five hundred years that they would be able to see the Messiah before they died, and he realized that even though the chance was beyond miniscule, it *was* possible for him to have the future Messiah in one of his classes. He felt he had mocked God by claiming that the boys were so bad that they were automatically unqualified.

"Aww, that's okay," I said. "I was just curious. I probably shouldn't even have asked the question."

"No, that's quite all right," he said. "But there is one thing that you are missing. The Holy Scripture also says that the Messiah will be born in Bethlehem. I'm not sure where all of you boys were born, but I don't think any of you came from Bethlehem. Now if you will let me go on with my lecture, I still have a lot of ground to cover."

I couldn't help it. There was a burning inside me that wanted to keep talking about the Messiah, and this latest revelation only made things worse and I blurted out, "My dad says I was born in Bethlehem."

Rabbi Friedman stared at me. I couldn't tell if he was mad or just deep in thought. Finally, after what seemed like an eternity, he smiled and started to shake his head.

"Jesus, you may be a Nazarene, and you may have been born in Bethlehem, but there are many other prophecies that pertain to the coming of the Messiah, and I'm sure that if you looked them all up, you would find that even though you are a good boy, and even though you live and were born in the correct locations, you are not the Messiah. Now can I please return to my lesson?"

"Yes sir," I said. But from that point on I knew in my heart that something was different about me. I knew that unlike the other boys in class who cared little for the teachings of the Law and Prophets, my interest in these things was growing by the day. I made myself a mental note to talk to the Rabbi as soon as class let out.

Class ended that day with no more talk of the Messiah. But as we all got up to leave, I made sure I busied myself so that I would be the last one out. As I reached the door I stopped and returned to the Rabbi, who was rewinding the lecture scrolls he had used for the lesson.

"Rabbi Friedman," I said, "I don't mean to bother you further with this talk about the coming Messiah, but you mentioned some other prophecies concerning him. May I ask what they are?"

The Rabbi smiled. Apparently having a student who was actually interested in his lessons overrode the fact that he was being delayed from leaving for home. He closed his eyes and leaned way back in his chair as if trying to collect his thoughts. Leaning forward once again, and with a soft voice and loving smile he said, "You see, Jesus, since the time of Moses men of God have written what we refer to today as our Holy Scriptures. These Scriptures, as you know, contain the writings of not only Moses, but of David, Solomon, Hosea, Isaiah, Jeremiah, and many others. In these Scriptures, there are many references to the Messiah, but it's not like the words are crystal clear as in 'The Messiah will be born on April the 20th, under a fig tree in the city of Bethlehem at the corner of Fifth and Main Streets.' No, the references are a bit vague and somewhat nuanced. For instance, when I said that the Messiah would be born in Bethlehem, the Holy Scriptures don't exactly say word for word, 'The Messiah will be born in Bethlehem.' Rather, they say

'But you Bethlehem, though you are little among the thousands of Judah, yet out of you

shall come forth to me, the One to be Ruler in Israel, whose goings forth are from of old, even from everlasting.'

"From this Scripture the Jewish Scholars have generally thought that this means the Messiah will come from there. It's the same situation when I said that the Messiah will be a Nazarene. Again, Scriptures don't say verbatim, 'Hear ye, hear ye, the Messiah will live in Nazareth,' but rather it says

'Then a shoot will spring from the stem of Jesse, and a branch from his roots will bear fruit.'

"This ancient Hebrew word, 'branch' (the Rabbi used his fingers to make the quote signs) contains the letters NZR that, back in those days, were the abbreviation of the word Nazareth. So you see, Jesus, it's not just a matter of pointing to five or six verses in the Law of Moses, or one of the Prophets, and say, 'There it is, this is exactly who He is, where He's from, or what He is like.' Instead it takes hard work and great effort to be constantly searching the Holy Scriptures looking for signs and clues as to his coming. Some people think that this is dull, boring work, but for those of us who are waiting for the Messiah, we love it. So, to answer your question directly—what are some other verses that point to the Messiah? Well, here are a few.

First—and I start with this one because it is the most difficult one to decipher—it's found in the scroll that Isaiah wrote. It says

'A virgin will conceive and bear a Son and his name shall be called Immanuel.'

"Do you know what the name 'Immanuel' means, Jesus?"

"Not really," I replied.

"It means; God with us. So what Isaiah is saying is that this virgin's son will actually be God. Try and figure that one out. I know you are still young but even boys your age know that virgins don't have babies. Another group of prophesies which are related to each other come from the writings of Moses, Isaiah, and Jeremiah. They all speak of the Messiah coming from the lineage of Abraham of course, but then they go on to say that after Abraham, He will also be from the line of Isaac, Jacob, Judah, Jesse, and then from King David himself. So you see, Jesus, we have a lot of signs pointing to His coming and even who His forefathers are in the writings of these men, but for the last five centuries, we have heard nothing. Not one prophet since these men has given us any more information. It's almost like God wanted there to be this long silent period before the Messiah would be revealed. Let's face it, when the Messiah does come, it will be the most significant event since the flood, or maybe since creation itself. Now, run along or your mom and dad will get worried that you are late. There's a lot of talk in town these days about that Simeon kid beating up boys your age and I wouldn't want you to get caught by him on your way home."

I left the Rabbi and stepped out into the blinding afternoon sun. The rest of the kids were long gone and as I walked home, my head swirled with everything the Rabbi had said. I thought how interesting it was that the Messiah had been promised to Israel by God more than five hundred years ago and somehow I feel this strange sensation that He is about to be revealed. Not only that; I was beginning to get the feeling that I might even know who He was. I felt a powerful affinity with the words that Rabbi Friedman spoke. When he talked of Moses and the Prophets, it was as if I somehow already knew them. All thoughts of taking that swim in Decoma Creek were gone. I needed to get home and talk to Dad.

Chapter 3
My Dad

Arriving at home I found my dad where he would always be—in his shop. Every day after school, I would work with him until Mom called us in for dinner. Being the oldest, I was expected to help him out in his business as well as Mom in the house. My younger brothers and sisters were too small to do much, so basically it was like the three of us taking care of the rest. On this day, I had more on my mind than carpentry work, however, and Dad could tell I was in deep thought as soon as I entered.

"Have a good day at school, Son?" he asked, knowing I enjoyed the classes, but my grades sometimes got me down.

"Yeah," I said, picking up a broom and starting to sweep the floor. After several minutes Dad broke the silence caused by my deep thinking.

"Hey, what's the matter, cat got your tongue?" Dad said as he smiled and sat down on a bench near where I was sweeping.

"Oh, I don't know. I'm just thinking about some things the Rabbi said at school today."

"Oh really, like what?" he asked.

Not knowing how to phrase my question, I simply said the words as plainly as I was thinking them. "Do you think the Messiah will come in my lifetime?"

My dad just stared at me. I could see in his eyes that what I had just asked had drastically changed something deep inside of him.

"Dad," I asked quizzically, "are you all right?"

After a few moments I noticed his eyes welling up with tears.

"Yes, Son, I'm fine," he said, staring straight through me now. And then, without warning or reason, he grabbed my arm and swiftly pulled me toward him. Wrapping both of his arms around my body in a big bear hug, he squeezed me tightly and for the first time in my life, I saw my dad cry. I was speechless. I started to pat him on the back as he slowly sank to his knees, still hugging me hard and continuing to cry. I couldn't speak. I was stunned. My big, strong dad was crying and all because of what I said. I felt so horrible, but didn't know what to do.

"Dad, are you okay?" I asked repeatedly with no reply from him other than a soft moan which mixed with his heavy breathing.

After about a minute, I could feel him slowly release his hold on me. He raised his head up and looked me in the face and when he did, I saw a deep sadness in his eyes.

"I love you, Son; I'm so sorry," he said, choking back the tears and trying to wipe his eyes with his sleeve. "I'm so sorry."

My mind was spinning. Why was he sorry? Why was he crying? What was going on? My dad closed his eyes and kept holding me tightly, putting his face right next to mine. I could feel his heavy breathing, smell his sweat, and then I felt his tears running down my cheeks. I just hugged him. I didn't know what was going on, but at that point, I didn't care. My dad had a lot of responsibilities working in the business and raising a big family and for some reason, he just wanted to cry. I held him and he held me for a long time. I never felt so loved in all my life. I wanted him to hug me forever. I didn't care if he was crying. I didn't care if he was sweaty and dirty from working all day and I didn't care what he was sorry for. All I knew was that the man I loved more than anyone else in the world wanted to hug me and kept saying he loved me.

Eventually Dad slowly began to release his hold on me. I slid my arm over near his face so he could use my shirt sleeve to dry his eyes, which were now quite red. He looked at me and with a shrug of his shoulders, which said he was a bit embarrassed for the way he was acting, he finally managed a smile. I smiled back and as he let me go and got back on his feet, he looked at me and softly said, "Son, can this just be between you and me? I wouldn't want your mom to know I was crying."

"Sure thing, Dad," I said.

With that I picked up my broom and went back to sweeping. Dad returned to his workbench and started to talk about things like the weather and the upcoming holiday. I knew he was doing this to get past the awkwardness he felt over the way he cried. I played along as well, talking and wanting things to go back to normal as soon as possible for Dad's sake.

Later that night, I heard Mom and Dad talking in the living room long after dark. This was unusual, as the house normally fell completely silent after the sun went down due to the exhaustion that occurred in both adults and kids from work, school, and play. I wondered what they were talking about. They spoke quietly, and Dad did most of the talking. I could tell it was about something very serious as I never heard them laugh or giggle once, which usually happened when those two stayed up late.

The next morning Mom made my lunch and put it in a sack for me to take to school. I noticed she was quieter than usual and assumed that it had something to do with her talk with Dad. Every time she looked at me she seemed to hesitate and stare just a little bit. I noticed she smiled when she did this, almost as if to say without words that she loved me. I didn't know what was going on but I had this feeling that with the way Mom and Dad were acting something in my life was about to change.

Chapter 4
The Beating

The rest of the school year took on a whole different feeling after what happened in Rabbi Friedman's class that day. Yes, I liked studying math, Hebrew, geography, science, art, and music; and most of the time, my grades were above average. But I loved studying the Scriptures. The more I read, the more I wanted to read. It gave me more joy to simply sit and read the books of Moses and the Prophets than anything else I could imagine doing. The Rabbi was pleased with my excitement and spent countless hours after class giving me special attention. Without realizing it, however, my pursuit of knowledge in this area was having quite a negative effect on the other boys in my class. One day, after an extended lesson with Rabbi Friedman, I left the school carrying my Scriptures and deep in thought. Meanwhile a group of boys were waiting just out of sight, and they had trouble on their minds.

"Hey, Jesus," a boy named Benjamin shouted, "do you think you're better than we are?"

Startled, I looked up to see about six of my classmates coming toward me. They looked mad and started to form a circle around where I was standing.

"Hi guys," I said, swallowing hard at what I could see was going to be a strong confrontation. "What's the matter? Are you mad at me for some reason?" I stammered, clearly revealing that I was scared.

A boy named Isaac sneered. "Naww, we're not mad at the little Rabbi boy. Why would we be mad at a brown-nosed teacher's pet?"

I sensed the circle closing in and I clutched my Scriptures tight to my chest. I had just used all the money I earned in Dad's shop over the past year to buy them and treasured them as I did my life.

"Hey, come on guys," my voice was really quivering now. "I just want to go home. Please, can you just let me go home?"

"Sure," one of the bigger boys shouted, "as soon as we lighten your load a bit."

Reaching for my Scriptures, he grabbed the portion that was sticking out over the top of my folded arms. He tried to pull them out of my clutches but because of how hard I was holding on to them, I was pulled along as well. His strength was much greater than mine, but instead of letting go, I was thrown to the ground—along with my scrolls. As soon as I hit the dirt, I felt the pain of several hardened sandals stab at my back and legs. I closed my eyes, as their curses and blows rained down on me. I didn't care. I was lying on my stomach and my precious treasure was underneath me, safe from their blows. I don't remember exactly what they were shouting but I do recall their anger at how they thought my studying and questions in class made them look bad to the Rabbi. They said that the Rabbi liked me better than them and he told their parents that they should be more like me. They went on and on, fueled by their hatred and jealously of me. I suppose that this ordeal only lasted a minute or two, but I really don't know how long it went on. I felt the blows to my back and arms as their sharp shoes hit their mark, and when someone picked up a rock and banged it on the back of my head, that's when I went unconscious.

I awoke in my bed. My mom and dad were standing next to me and I heard the doctor say that even though I had severe injuries I'd be all right in a couple of weeks or so. With those words he left the room. My head ached so bad, I wanted to throw up. Pain shot through my arms and legs, and Dad tried to cool my forehead with a dampened towel.

"Shuuuush," my mom whispered as she sat on the end of my bed. "You're all right now, just lay quiet."

I closed my eyes, and the towel that Dad had placed over my face turned the whole room dark. I began to pray. "Dear Father in Heaven," I remember thinking. "I'm so sorry that those boys felt that way about me. I didn't mean to make them jealous. I don't want them to hate me. I don't want anyone to hate me. I want them to love me. I'm so confused. I want to read and study your Scriptures, but I don't want to be misunderstood by the other boys. Please don't hold this against them. They didn't know what they were doing. They're just boys being boys."

As I was praying, I felt something inside me that I never experienced before. I felt a peace come into my heart and I felt like I was praying to God in such a way that he seemed to be sitting right next to me on my bed. I knew it was my dad's hand on my forehead, but I actually felt like it was God's hand softly caressing my wounded skull. I knew it was mom softly rubbing my bruised feet and hands but I somehow believed it was God himself who was doing it. Lying in my bed, badly beaten, I felt nothing but love for the boys who delivered the punishment, and now, the care being delivered to my wounded body felt like it was coming from God himself. I'll be honest, other than the pain, which I'll admit was pretty high, I felt better than I had ever felt in my life. I had peace in my heart because I felt that God really cared for me, and imagining the care being delivered by Mom and Dad was actually divine caused me to weakly offer a soft word of "thanks" to my parents. They didn't say a word to me, but just kept rubbing my wounds as they had been doing for the last hour. Knowing that I wanted to show them my appreciation, I said it again, thinking that perhaps they didn't hear me the first time.

"Thanks, Mom. Thanks, Dad." I said a little louder; still nothing.

"Mom? Dad?" I spoke a little louder, and the rubbing started to soften.

I was confused. I knew I was not dreaming. The pain made me aware that I was wide awake. As I raised my hand to my head I felt the gentle touch of their hands slowly recede. When my hand reached the towel over my eyes, I removed it and the light from the oil lamp on the table by the door revealed that I was in the room completely alone. I blinked several times to see if maybe my parents were in the room and I just couldn't see them, but I knew that this was not the case. My bedroom is small, and there is no room for anyone to hide. I then heard my mom's voice in the kitchen as she told my siblings to quiet down, because I was resting. My thoughts returned to what I had just experienced. I know I was talking to God through prayer. I know He heard my prayer. I know He gave me His peace. And now I know He was rubbing my bruised body with His own hands. I don't know how, but I know He did. Lying on my bed I felt like I was the only one in the world who was not afraid of God. No, I wasn't afraid of Him. I loved Him, and somewhere deep inside my soul, I felt He loved me too.

Chapter 5
The Gold

The next few days were hard, I'm not going to lie. Every time I moved, the pain in my arms and legs flared up and my head felt like it was going to explode. I can't imagine the size of the rock that must have been used to give me this goose egg but I knew it wasn't a pebble. Slowly, however, I began to recover, and after about a week I was able to sit up in bed and start talking with my family and eating some of Mom's good cooking. Now that I was on the road to recovery, my interest returned to where it left off before I got clobbered by those boys—to the Scriptures. In the days before I got the beating, Rabbi Friedman and I were having lengthy discussions after school let out regarding the coming of the Messiah. Of all the subjects covered in the Law and Prophets this one seemed to be the one that intrigued me the most. Gone was the Rabbi's irritation that once existed about discussing this matter. Instead, just the opposite was occurring. It seemed that every time I brought it up he had new and fresh Scriptures that pointed out details and clues as to the coming event. In fact, instead of me searching the Scriptures for these particular prophesies, he was doing it for me. He had written down a number of these references and I had stuck the list in with my Scriptures which now lay open on my lap.

Among the dozens of prophesies that spoke of the Messiah, there was one which I found most interesting. It is referenced in both the book of Isaiah and the Psalms of David and it alludes to the fact that when the Messiah comes, there would be gifts given to him, or most likely his parents. And these were not just small little tokens of appreciation. In fact, Isaiah says that he will be presented with, among other things, gold and incense. Now I suppose incense isn't all that costly, but gold? That's another story. Quite frankly, up until reading about the gifts that he would be given, I toyed in my mind with the unthinkable: that the promised Messiah might be from my family, perhaps even me. I know it sounds crazy; it's actually absurd to even think this way, but as the Rabbi was ticking off the criteria day after day regarding where He was to be born, where He was to live, and who his linage was from, I made mental notes that all of those could have been fulfilled by me. As far as being born of a virgin like he mentioned in our first study, I wasn't sure about that one. I was only ten years old, and to be honest I wasn't quite sure how that whole husband-wife thing actually produces babies. I know I'll probably learn about those things soon enough and I suppose someday that verse will make sense to me. Again, as I mentioned, it was that prophesy about the gifts of gold that made me dismiss the possibility of someone in my family being the Messiah. With the way money is always tight in our house I was pretty sure that we didn't have any extra gold lying around.

Later that afternoon, Mom came in to check on me and said she needed to leave for a bit to go to the market. She would be taking the rest of the kids with her and that Dad was working on a project several blocks away. She said she would not be long and I assured her that I would be fine at home alone for a while. Kissing my forehead, she turned and left. Several minutes after she had gone, I wished that I had asked her to get me a towel like the one I used yesterday as a makeshift sling for my arm. Knowing where I thought she kept them, I got out of bed slowly and in spite of the pain, made my way to the kitchen. I guess I never paid that much attention to these things before but the towels were not where I thought they would be. Maybe they were in the bathroom. Looking there, I only found small hand towels and nothing large enough for my purpose. Finally, I thought they must be in her bedroom. Entering my mom and dad's room, I hobbled over to the dresser assuming the large towels would probably be in the bottom drawer. I bent down and, trying to keep my aching back as straight as I could, opened the lowest one. Bingo. There were several large towels and bed sheets and I looked for the oldest one since I didn't know how dirty it might get if I wore the sling for a while. Down on the bottom of the pile, I saw an old sheet that I remember from years ago, and thinking that it would be a good one for what I needed, I reached down and tried to pull it out from under the stack of others. It was then that I realized that there was also a box at the bottom of this drawer.

The box was not very high, but rather wide and deep. It looked like it was custom-made for the drawer, and considering that Dad was an excellent carpenter, I knew he must have made this special for Mom. My curiosity was piqued and I wondered what Mom might be keeping in there that was so special. Seeing that it wasn't locked and assuming that it was probably some family records or perhaps a keepsake she might have brought with her when we moved from Bethlehem to Nazareth, I picked up the towels and placed them on the floor next to the dresser. I then tried to lift the box up as well. It wouldn't budge. At first I thought that Dad must have fastened it to the bottom of the drawer, but shoving on the side of it a little harder, it moved ever so slightly. I then realized that the box was not fastened down but rather the contents in it were extremely heavy. With that, I raised the lid and looked inside.

What I saw in the box was more stunning to me than anything I have ever seen. The box was divided up into three sections by wooden slats. The left section was filled with shiny gold bars; dozens and dozens of them. The middle and right hand sections were filled with precious spices and incense. I'm not an expert on these things, but it appeared to be frankincense and myrrh.

Closing the lid, I started to tremble. I knew what this meant and I was scared; really scared.

After putting the towels back and closing the drawer I tried to walk back to my room, but my legs were shaking so badly they wouldn't go. I sat on Mom and Dad's bed and started to cry. Then I started to sob. This isn't happening, I thought. There is no way that my mom and dad should have a drawer full of gold. If they did have this much gold, why are we living in this small cramped house and saving every shekel Dad makes for the basic necessities of life? I know why; because it's not theirs! It was given to me as a gift when I was born. The gold in that box doesn't belong to them, I thought as I sat trembling. It's mine!

To this day, I don't know how I made it back to my bed. I was so overcome with emotion and I cried so hard, that I must have cried myself to sleep. All I remember is Mom coming in and waking me up because she didn't want me sleeping too long during the day because then I wouldn't sleep well at night.

"Jesus," she said, "have you been crying?"

"Yes, Mom," I replied.

"Why?" she wanted to know. I didn't have to tell her.

Mom looked down and saw the towel I had used for my sling. She turned white. She knew that towel had covered up the box at the bottom of her dresser and she also knew that any ten-year-old boy would never pass up the opportunity to see what was inside of a box like that if he happened to come upon it. The day she thought about every single day over the last ten years had finally arrived. I just had one question left, and it was a big one. "Mom," I said, "what is a virgin?"

Chapter 6
The Big Night

Mom never answered my question. Instead, she slowly sat down on my bed, bowed her head and with tears streaming down her cheeks, she began to pray.

"Oh Father," she said as if she was actually talking to someone she knew and trusted. "Oh Father, please have mercy on our family; please help us, please help us, please help us."

My mom's hands were clasped tightly together as she prayed this simple prayer over and over. That's all she said. Please help us. That's when Dad showed up.

Dad took one look at Mom, and he knew. He looked at me and I could tell he wanted to cry again, but realizing that someone in the room had to be strong, he closed his eyes, took a deep breath, and let out a long sigh.

"It's okay Mary, it's okay." He leaned over Mom and put his arms around her as she quietly wept and continued to pray her simple prayer. Keeping his arms around Mom, he sat on the edge of my bed. He looked over at me and smiled.

"Well Son," he said, "now you know. Now you know what your mother and I have known for over ten years. You are the promised Messiah."

I thought the words would have jolted me more than they did. But, looking back, I can honestly say that since that day in Rabbi Friedman's classroom, when he talked about the coming Messiah, I had a feeling deep inside me that I had some connection to his message. Perhaps the Messiah might have been my brother, or maybe my dad, but I knew way down inside me that there was this feeling of kinship with God that I felt every time the subject came up. Then Dad started to tell me the story.

"About eleven years ago I was working in my shop. And one day, this beautiful lady walked by," he said looking at Mom and smiling now.

He gave her a hard hug and I saw her mouth form a tiny little smile too.

"She was the most beautiful woman I had ever seen and I knew instantly that I wanted to marry her. Being kind of shy, I just watched her from a distance as she made her daily rounds delivering bread for the bakery where she worked. One day I got up the courage to approach her while she was eating her lunch near the park, down by the river. I asked her if I could sit for a while. She said yes, and what started out as a short little chat ended up lasting the entire afternoon. Needless to say, it didn't take me long to "pop the question" and after getting the approval from Grandpa Jotham, we were engaged. Now Son, this is a bit awkward, but it's something that you must know. Before a girl sleeps with a man, she is called a virgin. This means that it is impossible for her to have a baby."

"I see," I said, rapidly processing this information and realizing the differences between men's and women's bodies that I had observed from the Greek statues in town.

"Do you understand what I am saying, Son? To say it is impossible is not an understatement. It is absolutely impossible," Dad was trying to drive this point home but overdoing it a bit, I thought.

"Yes, Dad, I get it. I know what the word impossible means," I said.

"Well then, here is what happened. One day during our engagement but months before we were actually married, your mom was visited by an angel and not just any angel mind you—Gabriel himself."

I shook my head in amazement and raised my hand for Dad to stop. "Wait just a second, Dad. You're saying that the angel Gabriel, the one who spoke to the Prophet Daniel and interpreted his dream for him, spoke to Mom, here in our little town of Nazareth, just before I was born?"

"That's exactly what I am saying, Son. He appeared to your mom and said, 'Greetings, you who are highly favored. The Lord is with you.' Of course your mom was very troubled by this."

I looked at Mom and she had stopped crying. In fact, she was looking at Dad as he told the story and was smiling and nodding her head in agreement as if she was remembering the whole thing all over again.

Dad continued, "Seeing that your mom was scared, he stated very quickly, *'Do not be afraid Mary, you have found favor with God, and I'm here to tell you that very shortly you are going to become pregnant, and nine months after this happens you will give birth to a son, and you are to give Him the name Jesus. He will be great and will be called the Son of the Most High. The Lord God will give Him the throne of His father David, and He will reign over the house of Jacob forever; His kingdom will never end.'"*

This is when Mom spoke up. "After the angel told me this, my first question, of course, was, 'How can this be?' I didn't say this because I didn't believe what he said; I said it because as your dad told you, virgins can't have babies and son, I was a virgin."

"Well, what did he say to that?" I exclaimed excitedly.

"He said, *'The Holy Spirit will come upon you and the power of the Most High will overshadow you. So the Holy one to be born will be called the Son of God. For nothing is impossible with God.'"*

"What did you say then, Mom?" I pleaded with her to continue.

"I simply said, 'I am the Lord's servant. May it be to me as you have said.' And then he was gone," she replied.

"And that's it?" I said, "Did he say anything else?"

"Not that day," Mom said, "But an angel did visit your dad a few months later. Tell him what happened, honey."

"Well," my dad started, "I was in my shop and right after my lunch, I laid down on my cot to take a quick nap. You know how I like to nap, eh?"

"Joseph!" Mom pleaded. "Please stop with the talk about napping and tell Jesus what the angel told you!"

Most Jewish women had a way of getting straight to the point and Mom was no different.

"Right," Dad said. "As I was sleeping an angel appeared. He said *'Joseph, son of David, do not be afraid to take Mary home as your wife, because the baby conceived in her is from the Holy Spirit. She will give birth to a son and you are to give Him the name Jesus, because He will save His people from their sins.'*"

"So what happened then?" I asked.

"Well," Dad continued, "for the next six months you grew and grew. We were all excited about your arrival when something awful happened. Caesar Augustus issued a decree that a census should be taken of the entire Roman world and everyone had to go to their hometown to register. So, being from the linage of David, that meant that I had to go to Bethlehem in Judea about 80 miles from Nazareth. The problem of course was that your mom was nine months pregnant and due to deliver you any day. I had no choice, but I was not going to leave your mom here alone. So, I loaded up our donkey and took some food and blankets and headed for Bethlehem. When we arrived after a very difficult and rocky journey, we discovered that all of the rooms in all of the inns were occupied. I went from one to the next and the story was always the same. 'Sorry,' they would say, 'no rooms available.' Then, we finally found one innkeeper who said we could stay in his stable. At that point I didn't care where we stayed as long as we had a roof over our heads and were out of the wind. That night, on a bed of hay, in the corner of a cattle stall, you were born."

At this Dad started to laugh. "Remember Mary?" he quipped. "The innkeeper's wife brought you some strips of cloth and you wrapped Jesus up in them and we used the feed trough for his crib."

"How could I ever forget even the smallest detail of that night?" Mom replied. "I was beside myself with wonder and amazement."

"Tell me more, Mom. What happened next?" I pleaded.

"The inn was at the edge of town," she continued, "and as such there were shepherds living out in the fields nearby, keeping an eye out for their flocks at night. An angel of the Lord appeared to them and the glory of the Lord was shining all around them and they were terrified.

But the angel said unto them, *'Do not be afraid, I bring you good news of great joy which shall be to all people. Today, in the town of David, a Savior has been born to you; He is Christ the Lord.'* Suddenly a great company of the heavenly hosts appeared with the angel, praising God and saying, *'Glory to God in the highest, and on earth peace to men on whom his favor rests.'"*

"Wow! That is amazing; then what?" I cried.

Mom continued, "Well, when the angels had left and gone back into Heaven, the shepherds said to one another, *'Let's go to Bethlehem and see this thing that has happened, which the Lord has told us about.'* And so they did. Leaving their fields, they came to town that night and they found you, me, and your dad sitting on the hay in the stable. They shouted to one another that this is what they were told by the Lord that they would find, and they left singing and dancing and laughing. I just tried to take it all in and remember as much detail as I could because I knew that this day would someday be here and I wanted to tell you as much about that night as I possibly could."

At this point Mom and Dad started laughing at how the shepherds were acting and I asked what I thought was going to be my final question. "What about the gold?"

Finding the gold, after all, was what led to the discovery of my identity in the first place.

"The gold and the other spices were gifts to you from Magi, who were wise men traveling from the east to find you. They saw the star that God put in the sky the night you were born and they said when they arrived that they wanted to worship you. It was quite a time son," Mom went on. "Nothing like it has ever occurred in the history of the world. The Prophets have been predicting this for forty-two generations, basically since Abraham, and it all happened on that night in Bethlehem."

"Dad," I said. "I have one more question. Why did you cry so hard when I asked you about the Messiah in your shop last month?"

I didn't mean to bring our little celebration to such an abrupt end, but this question sure did it. The laughing and smiling came to a swift halt.

"Son," my dad's lip started to tremble. "The Messiah is not only God's messenger, such as a prophet would be. The Messiah is God's son."

It got really quiet in my room at that point. All three of us seemed to be slowly coming to grip with what we now knew together. Mom and Dad seemed to have a weight lifted from their shoulders now that they had told me what they had been holding in for years, but for me it was just the opposite. One month ago I was a just a regular kid, playing games with my friends and enjoying the carefree life of a young Jewish boy. Today, well, today (let's just say) "changed things" and leave it at that. There is no describing in human terms how I felt today.

We agreed amongst ourselves that this was our secret. We were to tell no one about what we knew.

Chapter 7
Things God Can't Do

I returned to school a week later, and the boys who roughed me up appeared to be contrite. A few of them even tried to help me carry my scrolls as I was still limping pretty well. After a couple of days of this charm offensive, I knew the reason why: they knew I didn't squeal on them. It never occurred to me that I would anyway. When the school security officer came to our home about a week after the incident and asked me to name names, all I would tell him was that I just wanted to move on. He warned me that if I didn't tell him who the hoodlums were, that they were most likely going to do it again. I assured him that I could take care of myself and that there was no way I was going to snitch. After several attempts to get this information out of me, he finally gave up. For this, the boys were grateful, and looking back I think it's what kept me from getting beat up again.

One day, while we were all walking home together, one of the boys made a comment. "If God can make the sun and the moon, why can't He just make it so that we don't have to go to school?"

All the boys laughed and then one of them directed the question my way. "What do you say to that, Jesus? Why can't God just make it so we are all born smart, and nobody would need to learn anything?"

I smiled and responded, "I have to believe that our teachers wouldn't like it because they would all be out of a job! God could do that if He wanted to; but can I ask you guys a question?" I shot back. "What if God did that? What if He made everybody smart on day one? No one would have to go to school to learn anything because they would already know everything. Is that what you would like?"

"Yeah!" the boys shouted. "That would be awesome!"

"That would be awful," I responded. "Let's think about it for a moment. If everyone knew everything the day they were born and didn't have to go to school to learn, then lazy people who have never studied would be just as smart as you. They would be able to take your job away without having to learn anything because they were born that way. You would lose the satisfaction of getting good grades, because everyone would get good grades, and you would not be able to better yourself through education. Not only that but there would be no school to attend anyway so you wouldn't get to have fun going on field trips or playing games at lunch break. You would not be able to impress the girls with the knowledge you gained through travel and exploring either because, as you wished, everyone would know everything simply because God made them that way."

"That would be terrible," one of the boys said.

"Yes, it would," I agreed.

"OK, Jesus," a boy named Jacob muttered. "If you're so smart let me ask you this: can God make a rock so big that even He can't lift it?"

All the boys laughed. Someone shouted, "That's a good one!"

"No, He can't," I replied. "There are a lot of things God can't do."

"What?" yelled one of the older boys. "The Rabbi says God is so powerful that He can do anything. I can't wait to tell him his star student says he's wrong."

"God is all-powerful," I responded, "but He has set up rules of logic that even He cannot defy. For instance, God cannot draw a round square. God cannot make a triangle with less than, or more than, three sides. God cannot lie. God cannot commit evil deeds. There are many things that God cannot do."

I walked away hearing them mutter something about me taking life a little too seriously.

Chapter 8
Stunning the Rabbis

This is Passover week, and every year our family comes here to Jerusalem for this great event. We celebrate our liberation from the hand of the Egyptians by singing, dancing, and enjoying great food while we catch up with friends and family.

And we get to go to the temple.

Oh sure, I would eat the Passover food, sing some of the old Psalms of David, and enjoy meeting old friends, but what I would really love is going to the temple. It is there where the Rabbis sit and discuss my favorite subject: the Scriptures. This year is going to be special, I can just feel it. I have been studying day and night reading passages from the books of Moses, and many of the other Prophets, just to be ready. Being able to sit with the wise old men is thrilling to me and here I am.

One of the older Rabbis is speaking when I enter the temple. Out of courtesy, I wait by the door until he is finished. Looking around the room I can see dozens of older men, all dressed in their appropriate robes, listening, reading, or whispering quietly. As the speaker finishes, I spy an empty seat next to a middle-aged man, and slip quietly into the chair, careful not to cause a scene. I try to get up to speed on the subject at hand, and apparently they were discussing a verse from the book of Ecclesiastes.

"It's very clear to me," Rabbi Cohen, a teacher whom I'd met last year, was saying, "when the Scripture says, 'A righteous man perishes in his righteousness and a wicked man lives a long time in his wickedness,' that God does not always care what each and every one of us does on a daily basis. Some people do well and their lives are cut short by sickness. Others are very sinful and they live long into old age. It seems to me then that God doesn't always reward the righteous for their good works, nor does He always punish the wicked for their sins."

After the Rabbi made this statement he sat down, and the rest of the teachers began to debate this issue with strong opinions on both sides. After about an hour of back and forth, a weathered old man with wrinkled skin took the floor and seemed to summarize their final decision on the subject.

"I agree with Rabbi Cohen," the older gentleman said. "I've seen it hundreds of times. Wicked men living well into their nineties, and good men having their lives end when they are barely thirty. It doesn't make sense to me either. I guess God might have a plan, but I can't figure it out."

I knew I was by far the youngest person in the room. In fact, I was just twelve years old. But I felt I had something important to say, so I stood up and raised my hand. The moderator nodded his approval for me to speak.

"Perhaps, good teachers," I said, "when you are considering a person's life, you are omitting the part that includes eternity. In the end, both the good person and the wicked person live exactly the same length of time. It's just that one spends his eternity in Heaven with God, and the other spends his apart from God, in Hell with Lucifer."

The room was silent. The rabbis were looking at one another with quizzical faces. Finally, one of them spoke up.

"Who are you?" he inquired. "and where do you come from?"

"My name is Jesus," I replied. "I'm Joseph's son and we are from Nazareth."

Muffled laughter could be heard from the corners of the room. I heard one young Rabbi whisper, "Nazareth, what good ever came out of Nazareth?" But Rabbi Cohen was intrigued.

"That's a very interesting point, Jesus," he said to my great relief. "I guess if we use your logic, then the infant who dies in his mother's arms will live the same length of time as Methuselah?"

"That's correct, sir." I replied. "I believe that the scriptures say that each of us has an undying soul which God puts in us on the day we are conceived in our mother's womb. And so in His eyes, the fact that one person might walk the earth for a day and another for a hundred years is irrelevant. Both live exactly the same length of time: forever. This is why we cannot look at how long a person lives here on this earth as any indication of how God regards their behavior."

With that, I sat down.

You could have heard a pin drop in the room. I could tell that all eyes were on me. Some were friendly, as they danced with excitement. Others were glaring, and I could tell that I had struck a chord they didn't like.

Finally, Rabbi Wasserman spoke. "I think what Jesus has done is give us a different perspective of how we view God's response to man's actions. I, for one, would like to use this approach as we examine the lives of many of our ancestors. Let's consider Abel, who did all he could to please God by sacrificing in the manner he was instructed, versus his brother, Cain, who killed him. According to Jesus' argument, both of them are still alive and reaping the rewards of their actions—Abel in Heaven, and Cain in Hell. Is that what you are saying, Jesus? I just want to be perfectly clear before we start this discussion, because if it is, then we have a lot to talk about."

"Yes, sir," I said, "that's exactly what I meant."

From that point on, to describe the debate as a discussion would have been like describing a thunderstorm as an early morning mist. Rabbis on both sides of the issue were adamant in the defense of their opinions. Long into the night the debate continued. I listened when it was polite to do so, and spoke when appropriate as well. Eventually, I fell asleep on my blanket in the corner of the temple, feeling more at home there than any place I've ever been.

The next morning there were considerably more people in the temple, but the buzz from the previous night's discussion had died down somewhat. It seemed that the Rabbis had somehow agreed with me on this issue. It also seemed important to them to make an official statement, so just before lunch, we all signed a document that read, "Since everyone on earth lives exactly the same length of time (for eternity), then we cannot always assume that how old you are when you die has any bearing on how you lived your life—either good or evil." The words "can't always assume" allowed for the inclusion of Rabbis who thought God *did* reward some people by granting them long life or in the case of punishment, ended it early. We were now ready for our next round of discussion.

Rabbi Wiesel presented a study that he had just completed showing that if a person believed in God, and followed the Law of Moses correctly, that they and their children would be taken care of by God, and would never want for basic things such as food, shelter, and clothing. He ended his remarks with what he said was empirical proof of this by quoting the words of King David.

"I was young and now I am old, and I have never seen the Godly abandoned or their children begging for bread,"

With that he sat down.

I don't know why, but everyone looked at me.

Raising my hand, I motioned once again for the opportunity to speak. Rabbi Cohen granted it and I stood up and addressed the assembly.

"All I can say," I started, "is good for King David. He may not have seen the children of Godly people begging for bread, but I certainly have. What I believe Rabbi Wiesel has done here is formulate his position ahead of time and then looked for scripture that would support that position as opposed to using scripture as a guide to reach a position. My evidence is this: I'm using my own eyes. I know many Godly men in my town of Nazareth who cannot find work and have come to our home looking for something to eat. Maybe King David never saw these people but every one of us in this room has. I believe what King David meant was that even though there may be times when righteous people are hungry, most of the time, if they work hard and honor God with the talent He has given them, they will not have to beg for food."

Once again, the place erupted. Once again, strong discussion turned into vigorous debate. And once again, I fell asleep on my blanket in the corner having spent the entire day delving into the Scriptures. I was exhausted, and was out like a candle in the wind.

Morning dawned and the temple was now completely crowded with people. Rabbis from neighboring towns heard about the wonderful discussions taking place and headed over to witness it for themselves. Local priests and teachers who fancied themselves as scholars of the Law showed up as well.

This day, however, things went a bit differently. Rabbi Wasserman began by asking me if I would like to share something by way of opening the meeting. I said I would love to.

I rose and went to the front of the room and began. "Today, we are gathered here looking back, as well as forward. We are looking back on what God has done for us as a people, and looking forward to the coming of the Messiah. Regarding the Messiah, I would like to make one point very clear. When the Messiah comes, He will have been with God from the very beginning. He is going to be as intimate with God as God is with the Holy Spirit, who we all know spoke to the prophets of old, telling them what to write in the Holy Scriptures. This Messiah has been identified with God and the Holy Spirit, in the first book Moses wrote. And I quote:

> 'In the beginning, God created the heavens and the earth. Now the earth was formless and empty, darkness was over the surface of the deep and the Spirit of God was hovering over the waters.'"

I continued, "We all recognize that in this verse Moses points out that God was there, and the Spirit was there as well. Now here is where the Messiah is evident. It occurs in the very next verse when God audibly speaks those first words *'Let there be light.'* God's Word is the Messiah. There are three parties active in the creation of the world. God the Father was there. The Holy Spirit was there. And the Word, through which He creates, was there. So, my friends, when the Messiah is finally revealed to Israel, please understand that He has been with God from the very beginning."

It was then I heard my mom scream.

"Jesus!" she was standing in the doorway of the temple. "We have been looking for you for three days!"

Every head in the temple turned to see my mom, rushing down the aisle and straight toward me, Dad not very far behind. Honestly, I couldn't tell if she was mad or happy. Tears streamed down her face as she hugged me.

"Come on," she said, "we have to go, the others are waiting."

Tugging at my arm, she lead me toward the door. I looked at the rabbis, priests, and teachers sitting in their chairs, and I smiled, shrugging my shoulders and raising my hands as if to say, "Sorry, my mom says I have to go."

Out in the light and away from the crowd my mom looked at me shaking her head. "Son, why have you treated us like this? Your father and I have been anxiously searching for you!"

"Why were you searching for me?" I asked. "Didn't you know I had to be in my Father's house?"

Neither of them said anything. I don't think they completely understood what I meant.

Chapter 9
Ari

After we returned to Nazareth things started to settle down a bit. I no longer went to school, having graduated with grades that may not have been the best in my class, but were certainly acceptable to my parents. Now, instead of going to school every day, I joined my dad in his carpentry business and the two of us made a great team. While I was a pretty good carpenter, I was better on the business end of things—something Dad never really enjoyed. So most days I would be in charge of sales, estimating, billing, and accounting, and dad would see to it that the work on the jobsite was done, on time and with great care. Because of this, I got around town quite a bit, and invariably this allowed me to meet a lot of very interesting people. One was a young Greek man who moved to Nazareth when he was in his twenties, looking for work. He lived in Nazareth, but he always considered the country and culture of Greece far superior to this lowly desert town. His name was Ari, and he loved to talk. However, when I say talk, I really mean debate.

Sitting at lunch in a little outdoor café one day, Ari said, "Let me ask you a question, Jesus."

Every time he says this it's made to sound as though he is truly inquisitive, but actually it's just his way of starting a conversation so that he can debate.

"Okay, if your God is so powerful, while at the same time good, then why does he allow suffering to occur? Why doesn't he just put an end to it?"

He looked at me with a bit of a clever smile, proud that he had asked me such a tough question that perhaps I would just throw up my hands and say, "You're right, Ari! There is no God," or perhaps, "I never thought of it that way, Ari, maybe God is not powerful enough to stop suffering." Or maybe even, "Wow, you're right, Ari, He might be powerful but I guess He's not good after all." But that's not what happened.

"Ari," I said, "who are you to decide that all suffering is wrong and that God should put an end to it? It is very possible that a loving, caring, and good God wants to use suffering as a way to accomplish a greater goal. For example, a story is told in Scripture of a young man named Joseph; he was arrogant and hated by his brothers. In their anger, they imprisoned him in a pit and then sold him into slavery and misery in Egypt. Doubtless Joseph prayed to our loving, caring, and good God to help him escape, but no help was forthcoming, and into slavery he went. Though he experienced years of bondage and misery, which you would most certainly describe as suffering, Joseph's character was refined and strengthened by his trials. Eventually he rose up to become a prime minister of Egypt who saved thousands of lives and even his own family from starvation. If God had not allowed Joseph's years of suffering, he never would have been such a powerful agent to act on behalf of our people."

"Okay, okay." Ari was holding up his hands in a mock surrender. "I'm not talking about that kind of suffering. You know what I mean, Jesus. It's the wanton, horrendous, and inexplicable suffering that I'm talking about. Say, when a group of thugs indiscriminately kill a bunch of innocent people for no reason at all other than for the perverted joy they get from watching them die. That's what I'm talking about."

Again, he displayed a clever little smile; this time it was actually a smirk.

"Oh, that's entirely different." I said. "You don't mean suffering, you mean evil. If I may, I would like to rephrase your question. If God is all-powerful and is good, meaning He hates evil, then why does He allow evil things to happen? Is that a fair way of saying what you mean, Ari?"

"Yes," he demurred. The smile and smirk were now slowly disappearing.

"The reason God allows evil is because He loves us, and wants us to love Him," I replied.

"I don't get it," Ari responded shaking his head slowly. "If he loves us, then why doesn't he just get rid of evil so all that would be left is good?"

"I didn't say God wants us to be good," I continued. "I said He wants us to love Him. And if He removed our ability to choose evil, and only left us with the choice of good, then any love that we felt for Him would be false. It would be like we were puppets on a string. He would pull it and we would dance, unable to do anything other than obey His commands. That's not love, Ari. You can't command someone to love you. They can only love you when they have the choice not to. So, what you see when you see evil, such as the thugs you mentioned, is people who have a choice to do good or do evil, and they chose the latter. It's that simple.

"Now I have a question for you. Do you believe in God, Ari?" I asked looking straight into his eyes and repeated the question with a bit of a twist. "Do you believe in the God of Abraham, Isaac, and Jacob, who claims to be the one and only true God?"

"No," he said. "You know I don't believe in your god. In fact, I'm not sure I believe in any god. But my question was not about what I believe; it's about what you believe."

"No, actually, it *is* about what you believe. You used the word 'good' to describe our God. But you never said what you believed the word 'good' meant. How will I know if my God is 'good' or not—according to your definition, that is?"

Ari looked at me and I could tell he was trying to formulate an answer but was having a bit of trouble so I decided to help him out.

"You see, Ari," I said, "our Scriptures describe a holy, righteous, and otherwise 'good' God. We get our definition of 'good' from an objective standard—our Scriptures. Basically, we believe in 'Thus sayeth the Lord.' You, on the other hand, have no such objective standard. You basically don't know what you believe. So in reality you believe nothing."

"It's pretty black and white to you, isn't it Jesus?" Ari replied. "Good and evil; no gray areas, huh?"

"Look, Ari," I said, "we're all human. We struggle with lots of issues. I look around and see slavery, murder, stealing, and exploitation, and I have these same feelings of disgust as you, but I believe in a God that is holy and true. I believe there is a war going on right now between God and Satan. Scripture describes the source of all evil as Satan or the devil; and God as the source of all good. We humans are in the middle and each of them is fighting for us to love him instead of the other."

"Okay," he said slowly, "one last question."

"Shoot," I said.

"If God is good, and He is powerful," he was carefully choosing his words so as to not get hammered again, "will He ultimately prevail against Satan and evil?"

"Now we're getting somewhere!" I laughed. "That's exactly what He is going to do. In our Scriptures, you will read that God is going to send the Messiah, and He is going to crush Satan and His demons and they will be thrown into a place where they will never be able to cause suffering again."

Ari looked at me and smiled. "I love you, Jesus. You seem to know more about this God than anyone else I know. How is that?"

"It's in the Scriptures, Ari." I said. "It's all in the Scriptures."

Chapter 10
Lazarus

Growing up in Judea was hard. The Romans ruled their kingdom with an iron fist, and Judea was part of their domain. The market for wheat, flax, and wine, which was produced in our area, was poor at best since the economy was burdened by high taxes, corruption, and blatant mismanagement by Rome. But above all was the heat; the Judean summers were long and hot. Unbearably hot. There were times when Dad and I simply took the afternoons off to escape the sweltering oven known as our shop.

To escape the hard realities of life, as well as the heat, I loved to spend time with my friends. And I had three of the best: Lazarus and his sisters, Martha and Mary. Oh, and I guess I should also add—they had a boat.

There is an old saying that goes, "The amount of time one spends on a boat is not deducted from your total in life." I'm sure that's not true, but I will admit that when the four of us would shove off on any given day to sail around the Sea of Galilee, on the sloop named Arise, that those were some of the most relaxing and refreshing days I can remember.

The boat was old, but she was stable and could cut into the wind at angles that made her the envy of other sailors on the lake. We never raced her, but loved to pull alongside similar boats and, with a nod to their passengers, slowly overtake them and ultimately pull away. Every time we did this, Lazarus would get this little grin on his face that said, "Yeah, I got a good boat, but I also know how to sail!" Me, I would just smile and shake my head. I liked to sail. Lazarus loved to sail. The girls on the other hand couldn't care less if we were on a broad reach or running "wing and wing" with the wind at our backs. They simply loved to be out on the cool water and away from the hot desert sand.

One day, during a rather slow sail, the four of us were relaxing and talking about life in general when Lazarus brought up the subject of miracles.

"You know," he mused, "I read the scriptures a lot, like you Jesus, and I believe that God is the Creator of the world, and I believe the stories of how He led our ancestors out of Egypt, and all that. But I really have a hard time believing in the miracles. I'll be honest with you; I just can't come to grip with Jonah being swallowed by a large fish, Balaam's donkey talking to him, or even more amazing, Elisha raising the Shunammite woman's son from the dead."

"These things are hard to believe, aren't they?" I replied. "But you know, Lazarus, if you look at each of these miracles, God only stepped in when there was no other human alternative available. Take Jonah for instance. When he was thrown off of that boat, there was a possibility that the wind and the waves could have carried him in the direction of Nineveh. But if the wind was blowing the opposite way, God had to do something to get him there. So, He arranged to have a large fish swallow him up and deposit him on the shore. In the case of Balaam, he was greedy and wanted the bribe being offered by King Balak. The only reason God spoke through his donkey was that he refused to listen to God himself in the first place, and quite frankly the talking donkey saved his life. The Shunammite woman had her son restored to her because of her faith. For reasons known only to God, He decided to give that woman her son back. He was dead, and God resurrected him. No man could have done that for her."

"I suppose so," Lazarus said, adjusting the sails to get just a little bit more speed. "But if God did so many miracles back then, why doesn't He do them today?" I haven't heard of a miracle being performed for over five hundred years."

"That's a great question, Lazarus," I said, "and here is the answer. If you read the scriptures closely you will find a very interesting fact about miracles—something that is exactly the opposite of what you would expect to find; and it's this. When a miracle occurs, you would expect that everyone who witnessed that miracle would immediately fall on their faces and worship the Almighty God who just performed it, right?"

"I suppose," he hedged his reply.

"What do you mean, you suppose?" I responded. "Let's just say that I stepped out of this boat right now and walked across the lake to the shore. That would be a miracle wouldn't it?"

"Whoa, it sure would." He grinned broadly.

"OK, let's just say I did that. What would you do?"

"What would I do?"

"Yeah, what would you do?"

"Well, I'm not sure, but I suppose I would wonder how you did that. And then I would probably start to think about why you did that. And after that I would probably be just amazed and not know what to think. I guess I can't really answer that question, because I don't really know what I'd do. You seem to have a direction you want this conversation to go Jesus, what do you think I'd do?"

"I know exactly what you would do, Lazarus. You would do what most people do who have ever witnessed a miracle. You would be shocked and amazed. You would stand there with your jaw on your chest, and you wouldn't be able to believe your eyes. After a few moments you would start wondering what you actually saw. In a day or so, you would still be wondering what had happened but you would start to rationalize the whole situation. In a week, you wouldn't be so sure you actually saw a miracle, thinking instead you might have just been tired or dreaming. Finally, after a few months you would just think to yourself, 'I might have seen a miracle, or I might not have. Either way, since I can't explain what happened, I don't really try to understand it.'

"And that's it. That is what would happen if God performed a miracle right in front of your face.

"Now here's what *wouldn't* happen," I continued. "If a person who does not believe in God in the first place witnesses a miracle, they usually do not suddenly change their disbelief based on the fact that they saw one. Oh, they might be scared half to death and at the time of the miracle fall on their face in fear. But eventually, if they didn't believe in God before the miracle, they usually won't believe in him afterward. Look in the Scriptures. Hundreds if not thousands of people who were opposed to our God witnessed dozens and dozens of miracles, and the result was almost always the same. Ultimately the miracle they witnessed did not change their view of God. That's why God doesn't perform them today as He did in ancient times. That may change in the future when the promised Messiah is revealed, but for now people will have to seek God through searching His Scriptures and then after they have done this; decide to believe and follow Him or not. If they do believe and follow, then they will believe He did those miracles back then. If they don't believe and follow, they would not do so even if He performed a miracle right under their noses. It can change them, of course, but usually it doesn't."

Lazarus listened intently and in the end nodded his head. "You know, you're right, Jesus," he said. "I believe in God because of what I have read in the Scriptures. The miracles seem to be given when there was no other way for God to get His people's attention. I sure hope that I'm not like that. I feel bad now that I even questioned the existence of miracles. I know this; God probably did raise the Shunammite widow's son from the dead, but I'm not counting on that happening to me."

With that, the four of us turned into the wind and with the boom on the main sail swinging over our heads I caught the faces of both Mary and Martha who had been listening in on our conversation. Mary's was serene as she always loved it when we talked about God. Martha's face was quite different. She had a slight scowl as she had just cleaned the whole deck with a rag and was quite put out that once again Mary just sat listening to my words while she did all the work.

Chapter 11
If You Don't Work, You Don't Eat

He's back—my cousin Simeon, that is. The feeling of his finger being jammed into my chest was the first thing in my life that I could remember, and seeing him come through the door of our carpentry shop brought back those not-so-sweet memories.

"Simeon!" I said, surprised to see him after all these years. "How have you been?"

"I need money," he growled, not bothering to even acknowledge my welcome. "I need money now."

"Whoa, wait a minute there, big fellow." I said, surprised that twenty years later he was still as big as ever. "You can't just barge in here demanding things."

"Look here, Jesus," he was angry and I could tell he was desperate. "I used to beat you up when you were a kid, and I'll do it again if you don't give me some money. I know you and your old man have some because I see this nice shop here, and I saw your brothers in town the other day, eating at a fancy restaurant."

I knew that this was true because they told me they had seen him and that he said he hadn't worked in years. He also said that working was for stupid people, and that if they were tough enough, they could get whatever they wanted by fighting. We were about to find out.

"Simeon," I said sternly, "things have changed a bit from when I used to be your personal punching bag. In the book of Proverbs it's very clear, '*A lazy man hates work, and his desires are going to be the death of him.*' And Simeon, you are lazy. Now get out of here."

Simeon glared at me with clinched teeth and an evil scowl. "Why, you little twerp," he vowed. "You were always quoting scripture when we were kids and you still are today. I think I'll knock you down a peg just to teach you a lesson!"

With that, he swung a big right fist, straight toward my nose. But things *had* changed over the past twenty years. Simeon was still big and strong, but I wasn't a scrawny six-year-old anymore. Age, plus working six days a week, will do good things for a body, and the look of shock on his face when I grabbed his incoming fist in mid-air and stopped it cold was very rewarding. When I started to twist his wrist around so that it was now shooting pain up his arm, that's when I got my first look at a really scared Simeon.

"Simeon, you're a bully and you always have been. Now you listen to me, and you listen to me good. I'm going to be kind to you. I'm going to let you go and not beat you to a pulp like you used to do to me on a daily basis. And I'm going to do this on one condition. That you turn around and leave this shop, and go get a job like the rest of us. If you won't work, you can't eat. I know that's a foreign concept to you, cousin, but that's the way it is."

I would have let him go at that point, but he started to struggle, defiant to the end. So, I gave his wrist one more good twist to drive the point home. I spun him around so that he was facing the door and gave him a shove. He was big, but I was angry. I'd like to say that I threw him out the door, but that's not exactly what happened. Instead, the force of my shove was off a bit to the right, and he crashed through the window next to the door and went rolling out into the street, bleeding from a big cut in his right arm. He staggered to his feet and stared back at me with a bewildered look. I was panting hard and just glared at him. After beating people up for almost thirty years, Simeon got a taste of his own medicine and he didn't like it one bit. I suppose my friend Ari would be taking his side right now because he was definitely suffering.

I didn't enjoy my confrontation with Simeon. But I didn't feel bad about doing what I did either. Some of the Rabbis read our Scriptures and interpret them as saying that if we are followers of God, then somehow we need to let the world run all over us. That's not what I found in Scripture. However, there are times where I do believe that the Scriptures teach exactly that. This happens when a person is in a desperate situation through no fault of their own and they act, sometimes violently, out of self-preservation. In those cases, the opposite of my reaction to Simeon would have been correct. For instance, if a person who can't find work and has no money tries to steal your coat to either sell or get warm, I say give him your shirt also. If a person is tired from working all day and can't make it to their home and wants to spend the night, then not only let them do that, but feed them dinner and breakfast as well. The Scriptures and our Jewish tradition tell us that we are supposed to be generous to a fault, but with a case like Simeon, all this would do is enable him to keep up his evil ways.

Chapter 12
Hell

I had just delivered a proposal to a businessman who wanted to remodel his store on the outskirts of Nazareth, when I passed by a park. There, sitting on a bench all by himself, was my old teacher, Rabbi Friedman.

"Rabbi," I yelled. "It's so good to see you. How have you been?" I exclaimed running up to him. I could scarcely contain my joy.

"Fine, Jesus," he said, appearing glad to see me as well.

"May I sit down?" I asked, anxious to catch up on things.

"Sure," he replied. "I've got all day now that I'm retired."

"Retired?" I smiled at him.

"Actually, it's better described as just tired," he said with a chuckle. "And you, Jesus?" he inquired. "How have you been? I miss those long talks we used to have after school. I thought for sure you were going to be a first-rate Rabbi, but," he looked at my business clothes, "it seems you have found success in the marketplace, eh?"

"Yeah, I'm working with my dad in the carpentry shop. I love it, but I love reading the Scriptures more." I added.

"You always did like reading the Scriptures didn't you?" He replied.

We talked for quite a while about our families, the synagogue, Roman soldiers, and life in general when he paused and got really serious.

"You know, Jesus," he seemed troubled now, "you were the best student I ever had, and I'm not just saying that to make you feel good. I'm saying that because I think you might be able to help me with something. After all these years of teaching the Scriptures, I have a question that is causing me a lot of grief. It's the question of hell. I don't know how to put this but I guess I'm having a problem with our loving God throwing someone into eternal punishment. Can you imagine the trouble I would be in if I asked this question out loud in front of the other Rabbis? I'd be embarrassed beyond words. But somehow I think maybe you can help me with this question."

"Let's start with the Scriptures," I said.

He chuckled again. "Somehow that's what I thought you would say."

"It says in the book of Daniel," I stated, "somewhere toward the end, I believe:

> In the end, there will be a time of distress such as has not happened from the beginning of nations until then. But at that time your people— everyone whose name is found written in the

book—will be delivered. Multitudes of those who sleep in the dust of the earth will awake; some to everlasting life, others to shame and everlasting contempt.

"Let me guess, friend," I said, "you don't have a problem with people going to Heaven based upon what they believed or did when they were here on earth. It's just that you don't want them to go to Hell for it, right?"

"Exactly," he replied.

"Rabbi," I said, "many people struggle with this question. It's not just you. Let me see if I can help you out. First of all, I'm sure you would agree that our God is a God of love and justice."

He nodded his head in agreement.

"You would also admit that in the Psalms King David clearly says *'the Lord watches over all who love Him, but all the wicked he will destroy.'*"

Again, he nodded. Then I asked him a simple question. "Rabbi, what is hell?"

He looked at me quizzically and I asked again. "What is hell?"

"It's a place of separation from God," he replied. "And according to the prophet Daniel, it's a place of shame and everlasting contempt."

"Let's stop there." I said. "Even if that is all our Scriptures said about Hell, that would be enough to know you don't want to go there right? I've heard many other stories and speculations that have included a lot more than that, but I think it is clear that if you or I died and had to spend eternity separated from God, this would cause us more shame than we could ever imagine and our contempt for not following His ways when we were here on earth would be inextinguishable. Notice I said, 'our contempt for not following His ways.' Our contempt is aimed at ourselves, not at God. Rabbi, the path to Hell is simply a person's freely-chosen identity apart from God all the way into eternity. God does not send anyone to Hell. They choose to go to Hell. God wants them in Heaven with him as He describes in the book of Daniel, where it says, *'everyone whose name is written in the book will be delivered...to everlasting life.'* And elsewhere in the book of Deuteronomy where Moses said that if we want to follow God, we must love Him first. Those who choose not to follow the ways of God, or in other words, don't love Him, will not be delivered. This is not because God doesn't want them to be, but because they don't want to be!"

The Rabbi looked straight at me and with the most serious tone I had ever heard him use he asked, "Are you saying people want to go to hell?"

"I don't know. Let's go ask some of them," I said.

Looking up, I saw a young man walking down the road pulling a small cart full of vegetables, heading toward the market. "Young man," I shouted, walking over to him with the Rabbi following at a distance, "can I ask you a question?"

"Sure," he said, shrugging his shoulders.

"Do you love God?"

"What?"

"Do you love God?"

"What do you mean?"

"I just mean, do you love God?"

"Well, I go to the temple every now and then, and I try to follow the commandments, most of the time anyway."

"Let me make this real simple for you my friend, do you love God? Yes or no?"

"I told you, I go to the temple and try to keep the law; what is it that you want, Mister? Get out of here."

The young man grabbed the handle of his cart and stormed off. I turned around and looked at the Rabbi.

"If he can't say he loves God to a person who simply asks him a question, do you think he loves God at all?"

The Rabbi was a bit embarrassed by all this and it got worse when I flagged down another passerby. This time it was an older lady.

"Excuse me, ma'am," I shouted out, as the Rabbi tried to hide his face with his hands.

"Excuse me," I said as I walked up to her, "can I ask you a question?"

"Of course you can, young man. What's on your mind?"

"Do you.love God?"

"Do I love God? What kind of a question is that?"

"A simple question; do you love God?"

"You are very rude, young man," and with that she stomped off muttering something about "this younger generation."

"If you love someone, I would hope you could at least say so" I said, returning to Rabbi Friedman.

A third person walked by. It was a Pharisee, and he was clearly on his way to the temple.

"Sir," I shouted.

Rabbi Friedman, now grinning, just shook his head.

"Can I ask you a question?" I inquired.

"Young man, I'm in a very big hurry," he said. "What is your question?"

"Do you love God?"

"What!" He exclaimed. "I'm a Pharisee! What kind of a question is that?"

"A simple one, do you love God?"

The Pharisee looked me straight in the eye and I could tell he was furious at being asked this question.

"Now you look here, son," he said, clearly irritated at me. "I go to the temple every day. I tithe my earnings and I have never missed a sacrifice. If you think I'm going to lower myself to even answer your question, you are delusional. Now get out of my way," he said shoving his way past me.

What I said next stopped him in his tracks.

"Has the Lord as much delight in burnt offerings and sacrifices as he does in obeying his voice?" I said, quoting a prophet word for word.

"Why, you little worm," he spun around and snarled. "Do you think you can treat me like this?" and with that, he slapped my face hard with the back of his hand. The slap stung for sure, but I just stood there, staring straight at him.

"If it makes you feel better, you can slap my other cheek. But I would like to remind you that you said I could ask you a question. And my question is, do you love God?"

"You know what I love, you arrogant little ingrate? I love respect." And with that he took me up on my offer, and hit me again. This time I could tell the blow was full of anger; so much so that I was knocked backward and onto the ground. The Pharisee turned around and headed down the road. I got up on my feet, rubbing my jaw, and headed over to Rabbi Friedman.

"You see, Rabbi," I said, repeating what I pointed out earlier. "In the book of Deuteronomy, Moses said that if we are to follow God, and ultimately live with Him in Heaven, we are to love Him. I just asked three people if they did, and they got angry at me. If they loved God, they would have said so. The fact is, they don't love God. They are caught up in the cares of this life and have little time or inclination to actually think about what it is to love God. They do not want to love God. They want to do their own thing. So let's go all the way back to your original question. How can a loving God throw someone into Hell, which you described as eternal separation from God? Well, I think you have your answer right there." I looked at him with a frown. "He won't throw anyone in. They will walk willingly in, all on their own."

Chapter 13
Ari Returns

There must be something in the water in Greece. It seems as though most of the Greeks I know always want to debate. I think they have debates to see what subjects they should debate. My friend Ari was no exception. This morning we met at the same café where we were when he posed the questions about suffering and evil. Today the conversation followed along the same line. It seems he had a real interest in things of God, but no real interest in actually following God. Ari was not a lot different than most people I know, Jews and Gentiles alike.

"Okay," he started off.

I immediately started to smile. It was funny how every time he tried to challenge me with a difficult question, he always started off sounding like he was agreeing with me.

"How can you say that your God is the only way to Heaven? Don't you think that it's a bit arrogant on your part to exclude all of the other religions of the world and say that the God of the Jews is the one and only true God?" He looked at me and the smirk was back. I have to admit, when Ari wants to debate, he doesn't pick trivial subjects.

"Do you think I'm wrong by not considering someone else's belief as being legitimate?" I asked Ari.

"Absolutely," he said. "If you were really open-minded you would understand that there are many ways to heaven, and not just one."

"So what you are basically saying is that a person who doesn't accept other people's views of God is wrong?"

"Yes; I just told you that."

"Ari, do you accept my view of God?"

Ari paused and looked at me deep in thought. I could see he was trying to do the mental gymnastics that would allow him to exclude my way of thinking without being exclusive himself. Finally he spoke; albeit very slowly. "So if I exclude your view, I'm actually doing exactly what I'm accusing you of... being exclusive."

"That's right," I replied. "You think you are being open-minded when you say that you believe all paths to Heaven are legitimate, except for those like mine that claim to be the only way. By excluding my view, you are guilty of what you are accusing me of... being exclusive."

"I never thought of it that way," Ari replied. "What's the answer then? Who's right and who's wrong?"

"Now we are getting to the real question Ari," I said. "You are very observant. In order for someone to be right in this situation, someone has to be wrong. The positions are exactly the opposite of each other. There can only be *one* true God, not two. I'm convinced that the God of Abraham, Isaac, and Jacob is the one true God. Who do you think it is? And remember, you can't say all of them. Because that would include mine, and mine is exclusive."

Chapter 14
Andreas

"This is Andreas," my friend Ari said, introducing a man about his age. "I told him he could join us this afternoon. I hope you don't mind?"

"Mind?" I said. "I'd love it."

Sitting down at our usual table in the corner of the small café; Andreas, Ari, and I were discussing various events in and around Nazareth, when Andreas turned directly toward me.

"Ari tells me you are quite the devout Jew," taking our casual conversation in a decidedly serious direction.

"I take that as a compliment; thank you," I said.

Looking at Andreas' face when I responded that way, I could tell he rather meant it as more of a put-down than an honor.

"Well then, can I ask you a question? Ari also tells me that you and he have some great discussions regarding your religion."

"Sure," I replied, "but remember, it's two against one here."

"My question is this: isn't it rather unrealistic and self-centered for your God to condemn a bunch of people who don't believe in him, when he hasn't given them a convincing reason to do so?"

"That's a great question," I responded, "but first let me point out to you an assumption that you will have to defend before the question is even valid."

"What do you mean?" Andreas asked.

"Well, your question assumes that there must be a moral law out there somewhere that says you can't condemn people without reason. So basically your question is a moral one. Would you agree?"

"I suppose so," he slowly responded, trying not to walk into a trap.

"What do you mean, 'I suppose so?' Are you asking a moral question or not?"

"Yes," he snapped. "It is immoral for God to condemn these people."

"I'm very glad you believe that there is a moral law," I continued. "The problem with your question is that for there to be a moral law, there must be a moral *lawgiver*. That, however, is who you are trying to disprove with your question. For if there is no moral lawgiver, there is no moral law. And if there is no moral law, then your question is not even a valid one."

Andreas stared at me in contempt. "Don't try that double talk on me, Jesus," he shot back, clearly angry now.

"I don't believe in your god or any god for that matter. It's all just a hoax. There are no absolutes in this world, Jesus. All this talk of rules, logic, and truth, right and wrong are fantasies that people like you need in their lives to give them something to hold on to. Don't you understand? Everything's relative. If you believe something is true, then good for you. It may not be true for me, so quit trying to force your beliefs on everyone else. That's all they are, your beliefs and nothing more."

With that he looked away angrily, shaking his head as if to say, "Why do I lower myself to even talk to these simpletons?"

Even though he was looking away, I decided to continue the conversation. "Andreas, do you believe there is a difference between up and down?"

"What's that supposed to mean?" he answered, not giving me the courtesy of even looking my way. "Of course I believe there is a difference between up and down. Any fool knows that."

"Do you believe there is a difference between north and south?" I went on talking to the side of his head.

"What's up with you Jesus?" he exclaimed. "What kind of question is that? North is this way," he pointed straight ahead of him, and south is that." He said as he turned toward me and pointed in the opposite direction. "Up, down, north, south; what are you getting at?"

"Being alive, or being dead?" I responded. "Are they the same or are they different? Or to put it another way; is either one relative? Can, for instance, a person just be partially dead or partially alive, or are they in fact as mutually exclusive from each other as north is from south or up is from down?"

"They are mutually exclusive," he replied, glaring straight at me, "but none of this has anything to do with the fact that there is no god."

With our eyes locked firmly on each other I reached over and simply pushed his coffee cup off the table, sending it crashing to the floor; spilling all of its contents in the process.

"What are you doing?" Andreas screamed. That's my coffee you just pushed off the table! And you did it on purpose!!"

"Yes, I did," I replied, "but why are you upset? Do you think I did something wrong? Remember you said earlier that you didn't believe in right or wrong."

"This is ridiculous." Andreas fumed. "You can't compare something as tangible as up and down or north and south with right and wrong. Of course I believe in right and wrong, and what you did just now is wrong."

"Of course it was wrong." I said wiping up the spill and paying the waitress to bring Andreas a fresh cup of coffee. "But in a very small way, I just revealed a truth to you that you never realized before; and that is that every person on this earth has a moral standard. Just like they believe in up and down, north and south, and dead or alive, they also believe in good and evil. The question to you Andreas is, where did this set of morals come from? I believe that just like God created the world with a north and a south, He also created a world where there is a difference between good and evil. This belief is based upon the Scriptures that were written over a 6,000 year span and accurately and succinctly describe what God believes is good and what He says is evil. You called these beliefs fantasies earlier, but clearly you understand that there are standards. I don't think even you would consider pushing someone's coffee cup off the table as wrong, a fantasy."

"So where are you going with this Jesus?" Andreas asked. "What's your point? So there are standards, big deal."

"I do have a point Andreas," I replied, "and it is a big deal. You see the God who made the Standards that are clearly laid out in the Scriptures also said that following them will result in a person spending eternity in Heaven with Him, but not following them will result in spending it in an opposite place called Hell. It's a bit like up and down, north and south, life and death; as Hell is the opposite of Heaven. In the end God will judge if a person has met the standard or not."

"You Jews really amaze me, you know." Andreas said waving his hands for me to stop talking and listen to him.

"Your god is the right one and everybody else's is wrong. Oh, wait. It's worse than that. Your god is the one and only true God and everybody else's is just a figment of their imagination? Either you people are insane, or you're just plain wrong. I'm not sure which it is, but I don't want to be either, Okay?"

"We may be wrong, or we may be insane, but there is a third option that you didn't mention. We may be right. Maybe He is God, Andreas. Maybe He is the Creator of the World. Maybe He is the Moral Lawgiver. Maybe He is the Decider."

"It's just that simple, huh?" He said. "Well, I don't think your god is all that great if he throws people in Hell just because they don't believe in him or follow his standards. If that's the way he is, I'd rather go to Hell."

"Seriously, Andreas?" I pleaded. "You would willingly spend eternity in Hell than accept the one true God?"

"Yes," he said. And with that he stood up and walked out of the café.

Ari, who had been listening to this entire conversation without saying a word looked over at me, raised his eyebrows, and finally said, "Wow that was some discussion. But don't you think you might be a bit narrow-minded?"

"The road to Heaven is a narrow one," I said. "Only those who travel this narrow road will arrive. There is only one way to Heaven, Ari. The question is, will you follow it, or will you follow the wide way of accepting false gods— or in Andreas's case, no god at all —and end up in Hell? The choice is yours. You seem to be in the middle on this, and I've got to ask you: are you going to follow me or Andreas? We are going in exactly the opposite direction of each other. You can't follow us both. You can't go north and south, or up and down at the same time. You have to choose."

It was getting late and the sun was starting to set in the western sky. After settling up with the waitress we gave each other a hug and parted ways. As he walked away, I prayed that Ari would open his eyes to the beautiful creation that was all around him and ask himself those three simple questions. "Where did all this come from? Are there standards by which we will all be measured? Can I know the God who made both the world and the standards?"

Chapter 15
Silvio

Silvio was a Roman soldier; but he was also my friend. Making his rounds one day, he passed me in the park where I was studying the Scriptures.

"What are you reading, Jesus?" he asked, dressed in his full Roman regalia.

"I'm reading the book of Malachi," I responded. "Have you ever read the Scriptures, Silvio?"

"Read the Jewish Scriptures?" He asked, screwing his face up like that was one of the weirdest things he had ever been asked. "Why would I, a Roman, want to read about your god? Anyway, Jesus, you Jews should get out more. The whole world doesn't revolve around you and your god. Before I was stationed here in Palestine, I traveled to many countries and let me tell you, I encountered many different religions. And you know what? They're pretty much all the same. Maybe a slight twist here or there on how they approach their god, but they all preach love and after all, isn't that the most important thing?"

"Well, first of all, Silvio," I responded, "you should read the Scriptures because they are God's message to us. Not just to us Jews either. Many Gentiles have read them over the centuries and have come to know that the God of the

Scriptures is the one true God. Secondly, love is important for sure, but you can love everybody in the world and if you don't love, and follow, the one true God, you will go to Hell when you die. That's in the Scriptures as well. Finally, and this is really important for you to understand: No, all religions are not the same."

Silvio was rather taken aback by my serious response. "Whoa, Jesus," he retorted. "I knew you were devout but I didn't realize you thought that deeply about these things. It looks like I really hit a nerve."

"Well, actually you did my friend," I continued. "For instance, when you said that all religions were pretty much the same—can I ask you a few questions?"

"Sure," he responded.

"Did you find that all of these other religions believed that the world was created in the same manner, or did they seem to vary on how they thought we all got here?"

"OK," he admitted. "I did find a few of their ideas on creation to be quite different, so you're right on that point, they aren't all the same."

"And did you find their definition of sin to be the same, or maybe some of them didn't even have a concept of sin?" I asked, knowing the answer already.

"Well, I suppose you got me there. I did discover one religion in Asia where they pretty much meditate day and night and they don't bother too much with trying to determine right from wrong like you Jews do all the time. So, yeah, they do differ on how they look at sin."

"I thought so," I said. "And if they differ on how they view sin, they must also differ on how they address that sin; isn't that right? In other words, they must differ on salvation?"

"Well, of course!" he laughed. "If you don't believe in sin, you sure don't need to be saved from it."

"Do they all believe that when you die, your soul lives on for eternity?"

"Now, that one is a 'no' for sure," He grinned. "There's one religion in India where they think when you die, you are what they call 're-incarnated' and you come back as something else like a turtle or a horse. Oh, you could come back as a human, but that's not a given, so I guess you're right, it's quite a bit different than what you Jews believe."

"I just have one more question, Silvio, and then I'll let you go because I know that you are on duty. Do all of these other religions believe that when you die, you either go to Heaven or Hell?"

"No," he said shaking his head. I could tell that he was starting to understand just how false his claim was turning out to be.

"In summary then, all religions are the same except for the fact that they differ on matters of creation, sin, salvation, eternity, and Heaven and Hell. Yup, doesn't sound like they are all that much different to me." I said sarcastically.

"Now if you'll excuse me, my friend," I motioned toward the scroll I was reading. "I'm going to keep studying the one that I think is the correct one."

***

A few weeks later, I ran into Silvio again. This time however, it was different. Since our last conversation he had actually started reading and studying some of our Jewish Scriptures. He ran over to me with a big smile.

"Jesus," he said, "our last little chat really caused me to think about religion and how if I got this thing wrong, it might have eternal consequences for me."

"Not *might*, Silvio; *would*," I corrected him.

"So I've read several accounts of how your god... ,"

"... *our* God," I interrupted him again.

"I'm not there yet, but thanks for trying," he grinned. "I've read several passages," he continued, "and I'm really beginning to see why so many of you Jews have such a strong love for him. The Red Sea thing, the smoke-by-day-fire-by-night occurrence, and the Ten Commandments;

wow, that was really something. There's just one thing that is really bothering me, though."

"What's that?" I asked.

"Well," he seemed unsure of how to say what was on his mind. "It seems that the writers of all this Scripture were really just ordinary people in many ways and not serious scholars or holy men like I thought they'd be. In fact if I'm reading this right, many of them committed some really bad sins at one time or another and most of those sins were committed after they believed in God."

"You mean like King David committing adultery?" I said.

"Yes!" he exclaimed. "And Moses killing that guy, and Abraham lying about Sarah being his sister, and ..."

"Stop right there, Silvio," I said raising my hand for him to do so. "If you are looking for perfect people to follow, you won't find any in the Jewish faith. But the problem with your critique is that you are looking at the writers of the Scriptures, who were sinners, and not at the God they are writing about. Silvio, that is what this is all about. People, who are born of man, are born sinners. That is why they need a savior. That is what God does. He saves people from their sins through their faith and obedience to Him. Don't look at the sinners, Silvio, look at God, the Savior."

Silvio seemed genuinely relieved at this revelation.

"You know Jesus; I think I'm starting to understand your God. And the more I understand him, the more I like him."

"The more you understand Him, Silvio," I replied, "the more you will know He loves you."

Chapter 16
Captain Antonio

If ever there were a rich young ruler; it would have been Silvio's boss. Antonio had it all. He was the captain of his regiment, respected by his peers, and he even spent time in Rome, as a political leader of great renown. But Antonio had a problem—a big problem. He was always depressed and he didn't know why. Confiding in Silvio, who had recently begun following the one true God and as a result had a peace in his heart that shown on his face, he shook his head sadly.

"I just don't know, Silvio," He stated. "I should be the happiest guy on earth. What's wrong with me?"

Silvio quickly recognized that this type of question could easily be a trap. When your boss comes to you with a problem and asks your advice, you could end up having one of your own if you give him poor counsel. So Silvio did what most people do when confronted with this type of situation: he directed him to someone else.

"You know, Boss," he stated hesitantly, "I have a friend that I think you should talk to. His name is Jesus, and he seems to have some pretty good answers to some difficult questions that I have raised with him in the past. Would you like to talk to him?"

"He's a Jew, eh?" He came back with a wary reply. "I'm not sure I like the idea of talking to a Jew about this problem. What do they know about being happy? Most of the ones I know are more depressed than I am. Of course," he smiled as the thought occurred to him, "maybe they're depressed because we're here, eh?"

"That could be," Silvio replied. "I just know that when I've talked to him in the past he seemed to have answers—straight answers, too, not some mumbo-jumbo about feelings and philosophy."

"OK," Antonio replied. "Let's meet this Jesus and see what he has to say."

***

"Hello, Jesus." It was Silvio walking up to the park benches where we had agreed to meet. "This is my boss, Captain Antonio."

I could tell he was hoping that I would show the proper respect. "Nice to meet you, Captain," I replied, standing to shake his hand, showing that I did indeed respect him both as a person and as a soldier. "Care to sit and enjoy what's left of this beautiful autumn day?"

"Sure," he replied, sitting down across from me and inspecting me with wary eyes. "Silvio tells me that you have some rather unusual views on things, and he thought that maybe we should talk."

"Well, I hope they're not too unusual, but I do try to do what is right. Unfortunately these days I suppose that does make me a little unusual." I replied with a smile. "How can I help you?" I asked.

"I don't know," he started, "it just seems that a person like me who has it all should be the happiest guy in the world. But I'm not happy; in fact, I'm depressed." He said this while looking straight into my eyes and I could see he was not only being serious; he was desperate.

"That's because you don't have it all. In fact, you're not even close to having it all," I replied, not breaking our stare. "What you have are things, Antonio—things. That's it. You don't have what's most important."

"And what's that?" he asked sternly.

"You don't have a purpose for being here. You're living for yourself. Quite frankly, as satisfying—or not, in your case—as that might be, it's a far cry from what you were made for."

"What do you mean, exactly? Silvio told me you spoke plainly, so do so now," he demanded.

"Here it is as plain as I can say it," I continued. "You were created by God to love Him, serve Him, and enjoy Him forever. When you do this, you have a purpose in life that gives you joy, peace, and satisfaction that not only lasts until you die—it lasts for all eternity."

Antonio just stared at me for what seemed like several minutes. I could tell he had a dozen reasons he could think of to laugh in my face and turn to leave. But he didn't. He just continued to stare, and then he spoke. "How do you know this?"

"Look, Antonio," I replied. "It's pretty clear what has been revealed to all of us in the Scripture. And there you will find a wonderful plan that God has laid out for us to follow. It starts with an understanding that God is the Creator of all things and that His ways are far above ours. This should instill a certain sense of fear in each one of us as we realize that He is God, and we are not. The Scripture says that this fear of God is the basis of all wisdom. It goes on to say that those who choose to follow Him will find that, in doing so, they will gain a perspective of their life that is eternal, not temporal. Finally, they will discover when they *do* follow after the things of God that their lives are filled with joy, peace, and satisfaction that they could never achieve by focusing on themselves. And the best part is yet to come. If a person follows God, He in turn will bless them by taking their soul to Heaven to live with him through all eternity. Just think of that, Antonio; you could live a life of purpose here on earth and then a life of endless pleasure with God in Heaven when you die. If that doesn't sound like a recipe to cure your depression, then I don't know what is."

Antonio, who was listening intently to what I said, then turned and looked away for several moments. He then looked back at me.

"And what if I don't care to follow this God of yours; what does your scripture say about that?"

"Well, it says plenty about that as well." I replied. "First, if you don't follow God, you will follow someone or something—such as what you are doing now with your pursuit of power, money, and material things. This will lead to a very depressing life, as the writer King Solomon found when he tried what you are doing, only on a much larger scale. He wrote in the book of Ecclesiastes that he found all of this as nothing more than worthless vanity. In fact, he likened it to 'chasing after the wind.' But here is the worst part. If you do live your life for your pleasure instead of God's, you will not be taken to Heaven when you die. You will not enjoy the endless pleasure of living with him for eternity."

"What will happen?" he quipped, seeming to be quite concerned with this result.

"You will go to Hell," I replied. "And as great as Heaven is promised to be, Hell will be its opposite. The Scriptures say that it will be eternal separation from God and you will be in a place of endless contempt and regret."

Antonio appeared to be deep in thought when he finally replied. "I have just one more question for you. If what you say is true, then why does it appear that almost everyone, Jew and Gentile alike, is choosing to follow their own desires as opposed to God's?"

"The straight answer Antonio," I responded, "is that God loves us so much that He has given us a free will to decide if we want to follow Him, or go our own way. Unfortunately, as the prophet Jeremiah pointed out, *'A man's heart is desperately wicked,'* so the natural tendency is for him to fight against God and do his own thing. This is what you are doing right now, so I could ask you that same question—why are you choosing to follow your own path toward Hell instead of following God's to Heaven?"

"I don't know," he replied shaking his head. "I guess I never really thought about it."

"That's what most people answer when asked this question." I replied. "It's usually not because they have struggled with finding true meaning in life, or have been wrestling with this most important issue; incredibly most people don't even give it much thought. Can you imagine that? The most important question a person could possibly ask themselves is usually one they never get around to. Fortunately for you Antonio, our conversation here is putting this question front and center; right where it ought to be."

I could tell that our little talk really had him thinking. The façade of success was gone, and Antonio was now facing a decision.

"Look," he finally said. "I need to think about this for a while. I don't think you realize how much I would give up in terms of influence and authority if I told my commanders I was now following the God of the Jews. It would change my life completely, and not in a good way—I can assure you."

"I understand," I said. "I'm glad you realize that the consequences of following God will have a huge effect on how you are treated by those who choose not to. In fact, you will find that the people and things of this world will become strangely foreign to you as your focus will now be on eternal issues and not on your immediate personal pleasure. But I can assure you that if you do choose this path, you will lose your depression and gain eternal life."

"Well, I asked for a straight answer and it looks like I got one," he smiled as both he and Silvio got up to leave. "Thank you, Jesus. I now must go. I have a lot to think about."

As they turned and left Silvio looked back at me and gave me a wink and a "thumbs up" sign. I then heard him say, "Boss, if you want, I will be glad to share my Scriptures with you sometime."

Chapter 17
The Man of Sorrows

Walking home from work one day I thought how my carpentry job was slowly but surely fading into the background and my study of the Scriptures was taking over most of my time. I talked to Dad about this, and he said he understood. He told me to start taking even more time off from the shop now and really start focusing on what was to be the next step of my journey. When he said that, I could see it in his eyes; he knew my time was getting very close. I had been living on my own for several years and so every evening I was able to spend my time in prayer with my Father and the study of the Scriptures.

The time spent concentrating on study and prayer had a two-fold effect on me. On one hand, I was learning more and more of my Father's love for both me and all of His creation. I read how He longed for a people to call Him their God and would go to any length to protect and bless them when they did. I also began to realize just how much He hated sin. As a child growing up in a Jewish family we were always taught that God loved us and considered us His chosen people. This we felt very good about. Who wouldn't want the Creator of the world to choose you as His special nation? It's the hatred-of-sin part of God that got the short end of most of the lessons. As Jews, when it came to the fact that God hated the sin in our lives every bit as much as He did in the lives of the Egyptians, Romans,

Amalekites, and Philistines, and that as a people, we would suffer the same wrath as the heathens did if we didn't follow His laws—we didn't like it so much. But, instead of living lives that reflected this fact; most chose to ignore it. Now as I walk the streets of Nazareth, Bethlehem, or Jerusalem I see wickedness everywhere. This I would expect from people who don't claim to follow God, but from our own people, this type of behavior seems most disappointing. This observation has begun to develop a deep hatred of sin in my heart, much the same as it does in my Father's.

I now see sin for what it is—an affront to God's holiness. I see pride as man's way of trying to eliminate God from his daily life. I see envy as man wanting the things of this life to give him satisfaction that will only come from a close walk with God. And finally, I'm seeing religion as a stage play where actors go through the motions while they read a script that they neither believe nor understand. Take yesterday, for example. I was in the temple, praying, and when I was finished I walked past the money-changers who had set up stands by which they were selling sacrifices to the attendees. There was no remorse for sin. There was no repentance. There was no weeping for offending a Holy God. Instead, there was laughing, joking, teasing, and coarse language as each person tried to haggle for the best deal they could get. The circus atmosphere in a place dedicated to the worship of God was overwhelming to me and I grabbed a set of leather strips that had been discarded by a vendor and I twisted them into a cat o' nine tails. I gripped this whip with a fervor I don't remember having before and for the first time I realized that I hated sin almost as much as I loved my Father, and I wanted to drive it out of this place. I don't know why but I didn't whip those thieves in the temple that day. In any case, I can tell that each day I live I'm growing closer and closer to the time that I will reveal myself as the Messiah. When that time comes, I have a feeling my anger won't be abated.

At this same time as I studied and prayed I was also starting to get a clearer picture of what my near future looked like. I was starting to think of myself not as a Nazarene who was the coming Messiah, but rather the Messiah who was sent to earth to save all of mankind. The difference was like night and day. Instead of trying to find the good in every person I met, I started seeing men as they really were—sinners in need of a savior. I began to come to grip with the fact that the most righteous person in town was miles away from living a perfect life. A verse in the book of Isaiah played over and over in my mind, where he spoke for all of humanity when he said, *"All we like sheep, are gone astray, each one of us has turned to his own way."* I thought of how King David, in the Psalms, asked God in a prayer to keep him from his deceitful ways, and in another verse he prays for God to keep him from his willful sins. Over and over, men of God have recorded in the Scriptures how they are constantly being tempted to sin, and I have come to realize the tremendous grip that sin—Satan—has on the entire world. This world needs a savior, and that is where the verse in Isaiah really struck home. Because the verse in Isaiah that I alluded to earlier goes on to say,

> *"...and the Lord has laid on Him the sin of us all."*

Isaiah is very clear; the Messiah will bear the sins of the whole world.

And how must I do this? Again, the Scriptures are very clear that without the shedding of blood, there is no forgiveness of sins. Sacrifice must be made for sin committed; and I was to be that sacrifice. If my Father did not require sacrifice then sin would be left unpunished. If sin is unpunished, then my Father would not be just. He must punish sin, as it is an affront to His holiness. I now realized why my dad cried so hard when I asked him about the Messiah. He knew I was the Messiah, and as such I was sent to save the people from their sins, just as the angel had told him in the dream. Dad knew the only way to forgive sin was through sacrifice. He didn't know how it would happen, but he knew it would; and he knew I was going to suffer like no man ever had.

As I continued to walk along, the Scriptures I had studied since I was six years old came back to me in waves, giving me a clear and accurate picture of what I was now facing.

"Even my friend, whom I trusted, lifted up his heel against me."

"He was oppressed, and He was afflicted. Yet He opened not His mouth."

"He was wounded for our transgressions, He was bruised for our iniquities … and by His stripes we are healed."

"I gave my back to those who struck me, and my cheeks to those who plucked out my beard; I did not hide my face from shame and spitting."

"They pierced my hands and feet."

"He was despised and rejected by men, a man of sorrows and acquainted with grief. And we hid our faces from Him."

"And one of the soldiers pierced His side with a spear."

I am ready.

My Father and I are one. We have had this plan since the fall of Adam in the Garden of Eden. Now, just like Adam sinned once and the whole world was cursed, I, the man born of God, who has never sinned, will be sacrificed so that the whole world can be saved through me. The innocent for the guilty.

I smiled through my tears. Our plan would succeed. Satan will be crushed, and I will be reunited with my Father in Heaven forever.

But first I have to go to a wedding.

Chapter 18
Going Public

We got the invitation to the wedding in Cana and Mom, Dad, and I talked about it deep into the night. It seemed strange that after almost twenty years of keeping this secret amongst ourselves, we knew that this was about to change. I was now spending very little time in the carpentry business and almost all of it in both the study of the Scriptures and in prayer. The solemnity of what was about to begin weighed heavily on our hearts.

My cousin, John, had started baptizing people in the Jordan River recently, proclaiming that the Messiah was going to arrive shortly. In fact, I even felt the bonds between my family and me start to grow thin as I realized that I owed my allegiance to all of humanity, as they were in fact my brothers and sisters.

My love for the things of my Father had risen to where I communed with Him through the Holy Spirit more and more each day. There were some days in which the three of us walked and talked together without ceasing from morning until night. In fact, these days were rapidly becoming the norm, not the anomaly. I felt as though I was one with my Father, through the Spirit, and I was now prepared to accomplish His purpose here on earth.

Reflecting on all this, my thoughts went back to Rabbi Friedman who once stated that when the Messiah comes it will be the most significant event since the Great Flood, maybe even since Creation itself. Well, the Rabbi was right; it is significant, but far more so than He could ever have imagined. The plan that my Father slowly revealed to me as I grew from a newborn child to a man is undoubtedly the most significant event in the history of the universe. God, taking on the form of a man and living among His creation is one thing. But, redeeming them so that they may enjoy a close personal relationship with Him in Heaven forever is close to unimaginable.

**

It's time to go now. My hour has arrived. At the wedding in Cana, I will perform my first of many miracles, and Satan will be put on notice that his time of destruction is close at hand. The Jewish people have waited for their Messiah for five hundred years and now the wait is over.

**

I hope you have enjoyed this journal. But more than that, I hope you read the Scriptures. In them you will find the way to eternal life that is described in the book of Daniel that Rabbi Friedman and I talked about. Please don't delay in your search for God. Please don't put off until tomorrow the most important decision of your life. It lasts for all eternity, you know. The popular political struggle you may face will pass. The sports team you follow will someday be gone. The famous people that you love to watch will all pass away and what will be left?

Just you and your faith for all eternity. Don't be like those three people that I talked to near the park in Nazareth. Don't go walking into Hell all on your own with your fingers in your ears, not wanting to hear the truth. Read the Scriptures and realize what is says there.

I love you. I created the world and I gave you freedom to follow me because you love me; or freedom to ignore me and follow Satan. The choice is yours.

"Behold, I stand at your heart's door and knock. If any man hears my voice and opens the door, I will come in to him and dine with him, and he with me. And we will dine forever."

"I am the way, the truth and the life. No man comes to the Father, but through me."

"For God so loved the world that he gave his only begotten Son, that whosoever believeth in Him shall never die, but have everlasting life."

Post Script

This is a book of fiction. It is based upon a true story which can be found in the Holy Bible. I don't know anything more about Jesus' life than what I have read there. I do know from scripture, however, that he was fully God, and fully man. I know that he lived a sinless life and that he was sacrificed on the cross to pay for our sins. I also know, from Scripture, that he is coming back to redeem his church and if we don't correctly understand who he is and, because of this, falsely believe that we are saved when we are not, we will be left behind, and that is the last thing I would wish for anyone.

Acknowledgments

Generally in a book of fiction citations are not used in the body of the work. However, I acknowledge that I have borrowed heavily from many concepts and ideas that I have gleaned over the years from several authors: Ravi Zachariah, Phillip Yancy, Lee Strobel, Josh McDowell, Kevin DeYoung, C.S. Lewis, Rick Warren, Erwin Lutzer, Gregory Boyd, Chuck Swindoll, Francis Collins and Timothy Keller. Using their arguments I have speculated as to what Jesus might have thought and did as he grew into a man and ultimately went to the cross.

Finally, if I have offended anyone in the writing of this book, I am deeply sorry. For the life of me, I would not want to do that. I am not attempting to add anything to the Holy Scriptures, and sure hope that nothing I have written takes anything away.

Thank you for reading my book.

About the Author

Craig Wieland was born in Kawkawlin, Michigan, in 1959 into a family that traces its Christian heritage back many generations. After graduating from Bay City Western High School, Craig chose to enter the business world in lieu of college, as was the wish of his parents. A self-described "serial entrepreneur," Craig, along with several friends and family members, started ten companies over the past 35 years. This has included forays into real estate development, manufacturing, kitchen cabinet sales, engineering services, food service, and construction. Craig's experiences in business have given him a unique perspective on the world.

Today, you will find Craig at the Wieland-Davco Corporation, one of the country's leading construction firms. With offices in Michigan, Louisiana, Florida, and California, the company provides construction services to clients throughout North America.

Craig married the woman of his dreams, Jennifer Waibel, from Peoria, Illinois. Craig and Jennifer have five daughters and eleven grandkids.

Previous books written by Craig include *Pointed Poems; Tools for Teaching Conservative Thinking* and *What Conservatives Believe, and Why*

"Some will find this book "on the edge," others will appreciate the fresh and creative narrative about the spiritual formation of Jesus Christ our Lord and Savior. I think Craig's sanctified imagination gives us a realistic glimpse into that process. I believe this book will help you love Jesus Christ even more and may even assist in your own spiritual formation."

Rev. Mark Shaw
Calvary Baptist Church, Greenville MI.

"I like the way Craig thinks and writes. He always brings a different and refreshing perspective to whatever subject he is tackling. Using the personal vantage point of Jesus throughout his developmental years is a brilliant use of what I like to call "sanctified imagination." Woven throughout the narrative you will find a beautiful presentation of the Gospel along with simple answers to some of life's most difficult questions, including the problem of suffering, good and evil, the existence of God, Heaven and Hell, miracles, absolute truth and the exclusive claims of Christ."

James Moffitt
Student Statesmanship Institute

"Craig has written a very easy to read and comprehend book in "What was Jesus thinking when he was six years old". Anyone who needs a reminder of why we are here on earth, or, anyone starting down the exploratory path of discovering who Jesus is should read this book. It is very easy to get caught up in life and ignore the obvious path to eternal salvation, myself included. Craig has reignited my faith in God through this book and for that I am grateful!"

Kent Seggebruch
Businessman

"I thoroughly enjoyed reading Craig's book. He has created an excellent work that really captures what it may have been like for the son of God to grow up as one of us. He's done a really good job of weaving Biblical truths with what might have happened and in doing so helped the story of Jesus become real."

Rick Stacy
Pastor, Meridian Christian Church

"The storyline not only uses creative, everyday scenarios to illustrate difficult questions of the Christian faith, but it also uses that storyline to give Biblical answers in a simple yet cohesive manor. While most book written on such heavy subjects tend to be deep and complex in their approach, Craig's book speaks plainly enough for a child and profoundly enough for the exercised discerner."

Ryan Hoerr
Businessman and Lay Preacher

"I don't recall ever reading a book like this. It is refreshing to read a practical book about how Jesus may have grown up. You address some real issues young people face, and do it in a way young people can relate to. Great Job Craig!"

John Jackson
Businessman and Lay Preacher

"Fiction, yet so powerfully true...A biography of sorts about the life and teachings of Jesus - the only man who was simultaneously fully God. The story is told in a way that draws the reader near the heart of God, as shared by His wonderful Son. Intertwined throughout are solid answers to many of the probing challenges of the not yet believing. The message is compelling. The stakes are enormous. The benefits are eternal. May you be as blessed as I was as you journey through Christ's short stay here on earth."

Randy Gasser
Businessman and Lay Preacher

"Exploring the story of Christ in his elementary years, Craig Wieland gives us an expanded view of what life may have been like for Jesus. For the younger reader, this story will capture their imagination as they combine the truths of Scripture with the events of everyday life in a Jewish culture. Although fictional, this book allows the reader to contemplate the realities of a six year old boy who comes to discover he is the Messiah."

Joe Dabrowski
Lead Pastor, First Baptist Church of Okemos MI

"Craig's book teaches that "things" don't bring us happiness and getting work, family, and God out of order is easy to do. I enjoyed this book very much."

Dennis Forsberg
Businessman

"Craig Wieland has dared to bring the only God-Man, Jesus Christ out from behind the foreboding walls of religion, onto the streets of humanity."

Jerry Webb
Pastor, Flomich Ave Baptist Church

"I enjoyed Craig's book very much. Specifically I liked the prominence and place he gives to, as he would say "the Scriptures." Not only a lot of quotes and references, but that Jesus was always reading and relying upon them. I liked that he deals with hard questions (great answers as well)- evil and suffering, hell, God as exclusive, etc,.. and does it in a conversational style that works quite well."

Terry Stanaway
friend

"I read Craig's book and love it!!! It touched my heart. It made me laugh, then and it made me cry. It answered questions that I have always wondered how to answer. Most importantly it made me love Jesus more. What a merciful loving Savior we serve!"

Brenda Wieland
cousin and friend

Previous books by Craig Wieland

Pointed Poems; Tools for Teaching Conservative Thinking

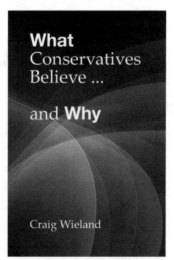

What Conservatives Believe, and Why

Both can be found at:

Craigwieland.com • Amazon • iTunes